Time Away from the Norm

Written by Mali Arena

Illustrations by Alix Davis

ISBN: 978-1-4269-7286-7 (sc)
ISBN: 978-1-4269-7287-4 (e)

Trafford rev. 08/19/2011

 www.trafford.com

North America & international
toll-free: 1 888 232 4444 (USA & Canada)
phone: 250 383 6864 ♦ fax: 812 355 4082

Dedicated to each and every one of you experiencing Time Away from the Norm – this really is for you

'If your face is swollen from the severe beatings of life, smile and pretend to be a fat man'
- Nigerian Proverb

With amazing thanks to Adam, Izzy, Frag, José, Julia & Pete – without whom this guide would not have been made possible

Contents

1. Introduction

OK, so you've been signed off work. Fact. This may be for a set period of time, or this may be on-going and dependent on various factors, and could pan out to be longer than expected. For some of you, time off may be great – exactly what the doctor ordered; a time to rejuvenate and replenish; some space away from the normal hustle and bustle; a time to really think and re-order your priorities. If so – fantastic. Enjoy it. Relish it. You're unlikely to ever have such time off again :). For others though, Time Away from the Norm may prove to be an incredibly difficult and tough time; to go from a busy and tightly structured week to effectively a clean slate of free time. Hey, you may not have even wanted the time off in the first place. But you are here now. So don't be too hard on yourself if you do find that despite all this 'wonderful' free time, you're just not enjoying it. That perhaps you're finding it stressful, frustrating... or frankly it's driving you up the wall with boredom. This is totally normal and understandable. If this is you, or maybe even partly you – then fear not, for this guide is at hand to provide support in the form of practical tips, advice and ideas to help you navigate your way whilst off work.

So perhaps you need a couple of ideas of what to do with your time or maybe you need a lot more help and guidance in terms of filling a greater space of time. This guide can help you. As well as those signed off work, this could also be an interesting and useful read for graduates, school leavers, pensioners, contractors, freelancers, the post-op, along with those who are job-hunting, on maternity leave or have been made redundant. Maybe you are someone who feels that you're on the verge of being signed off work or would like to help support someone who is currently off work. Whichever level and type of help you need, this guide is here to point you in the right direction. Because everybody needs a little bit of help sometimes.

Now the reason why this guide is so special and different from the rest is that I have actually been in your shoes – I have dealt with several months off work and been on the emotional journey that this consequently entails. I have been where you are now. So, OK I'm not a qualified expert, doctor, therapist or whatnot, but what I do have to offer are my raw, first-hand experiences and insight. During my Time

Away from the Norm I did a great deal: I spoke with various people, made numerous discoveries, came up with different ideas and generally thought a great deal. I now feel that I'm in a position to be able to offer my real-life personal experiences to those of you in a similar boat. And don't forget – this guide book is written on the sole basis that I believe this is something that would have genuinely helped and been useful to me whilst I was signed off work. And I'd now like to be able to offer it you.

The guide takes you through the journey of being signed off work – from the initial days, the time in-between, to getting back to work; as well as options if things don't necessarily work out. It can be read in any way you like – a snippet here and there, a quick flick when you fancy an idea, or reading it all in one big gulp. Personally, I wouldn't recommend reading this guide in one sitting, simply because there are a lot of ideas in here and it can be overwhelming to read so many in one go. And the last thing I want is for you to feel put off by this. So take it step by step. Scan a small section. Read it again. Maybe leave it a while and then skim through and find an idea you'd like to try out. What's also important to bear in mind is that you'll find that some chapters may be more applicable to you than others, whilst other parts may become more relevant as time goes on, and you may therefore prefer to read those sections at a later stage. However you decide to use this guide – the key is in really giving it a go and trying things out as best as you can.

This guide is primarily focused on those signed off from their workplaces and aims to get you on your feet, and to inspire and send you on your way. I know that some of the concepts are more challenging than others, but I also know that we're all different, and what I may perceive to be a perplexing idea, may be less or more so to someone else. And as you may have already found out by now, you will have varying states of motivation; some days will be better than others, and therefore some of the ideas in this guide will apply to some days, and others days they may not. The point is that they're all *ideas*. I also know that there are things in this guide that I would not have attempted and may not have had the ability to try. But on the other hand there are many things that I have had a go at and would definitely have tried had I thought of them at the time. So if it's ammunition and ideas you're after to help you be inspired, then read on!

Now let's get started :)

2. First Things First, Let's Get Organised...

Organisation is the key to keeping yourself motivated, and ultimately keeps you sane. It gives you something to aim towards in terms of getting you back on your feet and provides a framework and structure, which is often lost without the typical working day. There are many ways in which to do this, and here are just a few ideas that you can use, perhaps along with some of your own. Take a look!

Keep a Journal

This is a really useful tool in helping keep tabs on changes in your mood, feelings and emotions. It can happen that time becomes a bit of a confusing matter, and it may appear to pass much quicker or slower than reality. A journal records how you feel each day, and therefore gives you the concrete opportunity to view any changes and gets you into the habit of doing this. It can provide vital information not only to yourself, but also to health professionals, your workplace and generally to those around you, as you have a clear point of reference to refer to when being asked how you are doing. And remember – small achievements really do add up (to large amounts!), and there's nothing quite like reading an entry from several months ago, and realising how that situation has changed and progressed for the better. And if things haven't improved, then a journal allows you to spot patterns and draw links that could later enable you to change and improve things. Winner all round, I say.

Additionally, a journal forces you to reflect, record, and deliberately notice how you are feeling and acknowledge the small changes taking place. You can write anything from a couple of words to several paragraphs, and update this as often as you like – several times a day even – whatever thoughts come to you. The point is to actively raise your awareness of how you feel, which by acknowledging your emotional state can help you work to overcome it. Give it a whirl ;).

Dear Diary

As well as keeping a journal, a diary is also essential to record any important dates, be it a return-to-work interview, occupational health meeting or a doctor's appointment – all these dates are likely to be important, and a diary is a simple way to keep them all recorded in one place. Foolproof :). Also don't forget your Nan's birthday, your best friend's wedding and all those other really important dates that you may be finding difficult to remember with other things potentially going round in your head. It's essential not to forget these other dates, as they're key to keeping you in touch and together with the rest of

6

your life and those in it. And not to mention the fact that it's actually quite nice to wish someone good luck for an important job interview or if they're having their tonsils taken out. Nice!

As with anything that involves writing things down, diaries aren't just great for dotting in those various appointments we all face. They're also great for having a rant! Yes, diary writing has been proven to be highly therapeutic and really does help clear your head or get something off your chest. I personally find writing stuff down to be amazing, simply because when you write, you are really forced to clarify things, and to do this effectively you need to detach yourself from the situation. It truly works a treat.

Perhaps you want to write about three things that went well at the end of each day, why you think they went well and what you are grateful for in life. Now this last one is an interesting one. I remember reading about how we should express gratitude; how it's a good habit to get into, and thinking 'how lame is that – does anyone *actually* sit-down and do this...?!' And now I do it. Not every day, but once in a while when I'm not feeling my best, or if I'm in 'victim mode' and feeling a tad sorry for myself, I do it. And there really is so much stuff to be thankful for, even when you think that there's nada.

Again, you can write as much or as little as you like; write about your day, write about others around you, whatever takes your fancy really. Like anything, it becomes easier the more you do it, as it becomes that bit more natural and habitual over time. Try it.

Schedule it in!

A timetable can be as detailed or as brief as you like – a couple of lines and notes jotted down on the back of a kitchen towel each day, or an elaborate version which automatically updates itself for the upcoming year. The idea here is just to provide some kind of framework for your time off and to ensure that you are doing things on a day-to-day basis – that you are thinking ahead and planning to do things and booking them in where necessary. Sometimes for activities that look a bit sketchy, it's worth having a backup plan; a plan B if it doesn't go as scheduled, so that either way you'll end up doing *something*. It also gets your mind thinking of ideas and opportunities that bit more, and keeps the brain active! Bonus.

Now, it's vitally important to stick with what you've planned and to make every effort to meet these commitments. And I know that sometimes you'll feel like you'd rather not bother; it's easier to do nothing, as everything just feels like one great big Mount Everest style effort. I can assure you; this feeling will only get worse. As awful as that sounds, it really is worth making that bit of effort and truly pushing yourself. Nobody said it was going to be easy... But you will find that over time, as you begin to live out your new Norm (because that's what we're creating here), the easier it becomes. As with work or university or any other routine you've had in your life, it becomes the new Norm and you learn to live by it. If anything, the Norm we are creating here is a special Norm, as it's *your* new Norm and you get to make it as varied and as exciting, or as chilled and relaxed as you'd like it to be. Go create!

Another key, as with any kind of planning, is to make it realistic. There's no point overloading yourself with cake baking, card making, shopping trip, a lunch date, trip to the museum and a jog round your local park all booked in for a Tuesday afternoon. Trust me; I made this mistake once before – it got a tad hectic to say the least...! Start off small. Start off tiny if you like. And then build on this foundation. And just totally go at your own pace. And although I've stressed that it's really important to stick with your plan, don't be too harsh on yourself if something doesn't happen; if someone cancels lunch with you at the last minute, if the exhibition you wanted to see has been closed due to maintenance or if your train has been severely delayed (it is the UK, after all!). Whatever's happened, you've given it a go, and that's what counts. These things happen, and they certainly shouldn't hinder you from carrying on with what you're already doing – you're doing a damn good job ;).

And if you are one of those people who can spontaneously live by the day and decide when you wake up what you'll do for the day, and naturally go along with the flow of things... then I'm very jealous of you! Seriously though, if you are like this, and therefore feel that a timetable doesn't apply, then that's fine. I'd still recommend having some kind of schedule though, even if it's just a very loose one, and then going along and changing it as you like. Another thing that might perhaps be useful is having a list of different activities you'd like to do, so even if you don't wish to plan exactly what you'll be doing and when, but find yourself at a loose end – you can have a look at your list of ideas, and crack right on with it!

Create an Action Plan

During my Time Away from the Norm, I personally found this to be one of the best ways to turn my thoughts and ideas into something real and actionable. Often it is the case that you have all of these concepts and intentions that are spinning around in your mind, but they aren't written down and therefore not part of anything tangible. The sigh of relief you will feel when you complete an action plan (or getting any kind of thought to paper) is remarkable – actually putting pen to paper (or finger to keyboard) can make a huge difference and helps rest your head a bit from all that thinking. The next couple of pages show an example of one that I used, and this can be amended as desired. Feel free to do this – add in a couple of pictures, a few polka dots, some music – really make it your own ;).

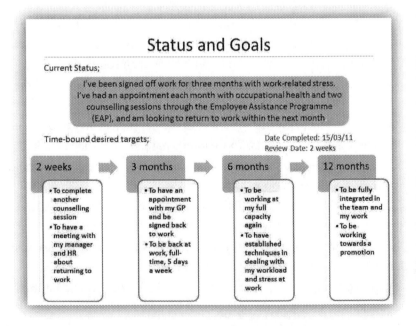

Action Plan – Getting Back to Work

Problem	Desired Result	Actions + Responsibility	Action Date	Comments
Feeling detached from the team / not knowing what has been happening / feeling that I've missed out on a huge chunk of time away from work	To feel involved and part of the team again	- Being sent useful news and slides to my email account, e.g. 'Marketing Latest', slides from the team meeting and any newsletters distributed. *Manager* to *action*	ASAP	
		- Reading work related articles / news-sites, e.g. Marketing Week	On-going	

Action Plan – What am I Doing?

Action	Desired Outcome	Action Date	Comments / Progress
To have 3 creative based projects to work on (photography, a sculpture, scrapbook)	To maintain hobbies / interests and to use this as a type of art therapy, as recommended by the *Doctor*	On-going – daily	This is going well, and I'm finding it relaxing
On-line CBT	To learn CBT techniques and apply them to my thoughts to solve problems through a goal-orientated, systematic approach	On-going – weekly	I've learnt two new techniques I think I can really use
Seek voluntary work	To further establish a routine to get used to going back to work and to provide structure to my time away from work	18th March	I will be meeting with the local voluntary centre
Work from home	To ease my-self back into work-related tasks and to establish a routine around this	On-going	Ask *Manager* for feedback on my work
Weekly updates to *Manager*	To inform *Manager* of my whereabouts and generally inform what I'm doing	Weekly	Started 10/03/11
Undertake regular exercise	To combat stress / anxiety, and to increase my health and fitness levels	On-going – 3 times a week	

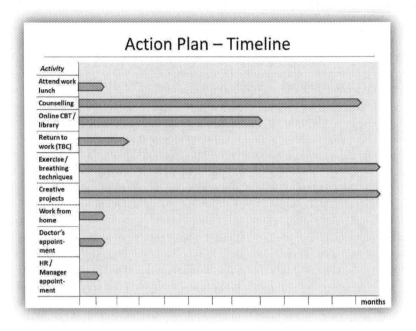

Once you complete your action plan, you can do whatever you like with it! You can keep it to yourself – review it every couple of weeks; update the goals, action points and timeline and monitor how you're progressing and generally getting on. That's absolutely fine. If you like, you can send it to your line manager or another trusted colleague so you have someone in your workplace to work with you on it, which is especially useful if the plan is focusing on getting you back to work, as in the example. It may also be the case that you need someone from a work point of view to help action some of the points, so this could be a really good idea. Alternatively, you may like to work on the plan with a friend or partner, or perhaps a doctor or another professional you're working with. One of the benefits of sharing the action plan with another person is that you're more likely to do it! I guess it makes it more real to have a conversation out loud about it. It also helps to have the other person review the plan to check that it is realistic and achievable for you. And if you find the action plan to be useful, you can even create an alternative copy for your personal life (just keep the two plans clearly labelled!), as well as any other versions you wish to create that you feel would be of benefit to you.

Be Inspired!

Everyone needs a bit of inspiration from time to time, and a great way of making sure you have this available at your fingertips is by creating your very own 'Inspiration' book. The point here is that whenever you hear something inspiring – a lyric, an idea, a positive thought, a place to go and see – absolutely *anything* that you find motivating, then jot it down! You can write it in a notebook or a post-it note at the time of inspiration – save up the notes and then paste them into your book, so you keep them all in one central place. Include photos and postcards too. This also works with compliments you receive – if someone's told you the report you wrote is really interesting; your tie looks nice; you look 30 when you're actually 40(!); your new barnet suits you – whatever it is – make a note of it! And you really can make this up as you go along, and do it however you like. Maybe make notes of places where you feel happy and content at, and visit those places when you are feeling low and you need that Oomph back in you, perhaps. Essentially, what you'll have as you go along is ammunition – inspiring, feel-good ammunition that you can dip in and out of when needed. So if you're not feeling tip-top and you need a boost, then grab your 'Inspiration' book and have a read through – it'll help make you feel that bit better. Do give it a go!

Arena's Top-Tip Chapter Summary

✓ Keep tabs on your emotions on a regular basis by jotting down how you feel in a handy-sized journal

✓ Keep note of the important dates, but also let it all out in a brawl-sized rant in the private bounds of your diary

✓ Turn your day into something tangible – make a realistic timetable to provide structure to your time off that you endeavour to stick with

✓ Make an action plan of your current status and goals, and ultimately make them happen through step-by-step action points that you decide on

✓ Make inspiration a reality whenever you seek it – have your own positive thoughts and pick-ups available in your very own 'Inspiration' book

3. Social Time

During your time off, it's important to keep a sense of social life alive, as often this is something that can have a big impact on your mood, and when lacking, can really make you feel distanced from others and the world around you. When experiencing Time Away from the Norm, it can take that bit of extra effort to find social things to do. But, as ever, worry not, for this guide is at hand and is armed with different ways to enable you to achieve just that! Read on :).

The Virtual Community

Gumtree (www.gumtree.com) is a website community filled with ads on everything from pets, housing, dating to jobs, and has localised websites for numerous towns and cities around the country. The site gives you a range of opportunities to meet with people (often those you wouldn't normally have the chance to meet), make new friends and generally help you with your Time Away from the Norm. You can exchange skills, stories, learn something completely new, pick up a rideshare or join a sports team – and these are literally just a handful of ideas that the wonderful world of Gumtree can introduce to you! It's good just to head onto the website and have a bit of a browse to see what floats your boat. And remember, Gumtree is just one of the sites that you can use – www.meetup.com is another, and there are many others out there. Don't forget – you really aren't the only one facing Time Away from the Norm, and there's a whole lot going on out there! It may even be worth Googling meet ups in your local area, as what's available may vary depending on where you are based around the country. Imagine all the exciting new things you can learn, the fantastic new people you could meet and then telling those around you what you've been up to in the week?! Jea-lous ;)!

Social Network it

Social networking's great. I agree. But sometimes it can give out the wrong impression that you really don't intend to give out. I, for instance, had some photos up from a while back, looking all merry, having the time of my life and with varied comments below the pictures, it was inevitably on the latest news feed for quite some time. The pictures were taken some time ago, but I guess I looked the same. And I know those around me knew that my life was a million miles away from my life at the time of the photos. However, if your work colleagues and other unsuspecting persons stumble upon the pictures, and they're struggling with their workload and possibly resenting you for not being at work, they may not have the same opinion and understanding, so it's worth keeping this in mind.

Now I'm not advocating deleting all your work colleagues off your social networking sites, as this may also give out the wrong impression. But perhaps limiting what people can see, changing privacy settings or just generally keeping an eye on what's on your profile can help make a difference. And obviously if you are managing to have the time of your life during your Time Away from the Norm – good on you! This is great medicine for you and exactly what the doctor ordered, so relish it – it's your time off and you can do whatever you like with it. But do just *think* about the impression such pictures can give, and about your colleagues when you'll re-join them again. Just one of those things to be aware of I guess.

By bearing these simple guidelines in mind, don't forget that social networking can offer many plus points! It helps you find out who's in town, enables you to get back in touch with those long lost connections, should you wish to – be it old school friends, an old gym partner, that girl you always thought was quite cute or an old work colleague perhaps. Whoever they are, they're likely to be on some kind of networking site. And it really does make staying in touch that bit easier – instead of sitting down and writing out an entire email to someone, you can quickly remark on a picture, 'like' a comment or quickly jot on several statuses at the same time. Genius! It also keeps you involved and a part of a community, as well as enabling you to easily show that you are thinking of someone. Obviously, it's no substitute for actually seeing or speaking with someone, you know that, but it's another way to stay in touch and an easy way to do just that. Plus, don't forget the more traditional ways of staying in touch online – messenger, chat, Skype and the good ol' webcam. Stay happily connected!

ET Phone Home

ET's an amazing film, isn't it? OK, so aside from a stroll down Nostalgia Street and watching ET again, you could also pick up the phone and actually call and speak to those you haven't spoken to in a while. Also don't forget to *continue* speaking to those you already chat to on a regular basis or maybe just call that person who has the incredible ability to cheer you up no end. As all the telecom and mobile phone companies will tell us, keeping in touch is vitally important, and although they have other agendas, there is truthfully nothing like speaking to someone and having a good ol' convo and catch-up with them. If anything, it's more crucial to continue doing this when experiencing Time Away from the Norm – not just because you have more time to, but because if you're finding things tough, then you're likely to need the support of people around you to help you through these difficult times.

Talking to others can also provide you with encouragement, advice, a whole new perspective on things or simply a pick-up by having a listening ear at the other end of the line. It really can make all the difference. And OK, you're feeling great today, and you may not need that booster chat, but what if tomorrow's slightly different and you could really do with a friendly call? Now, I'm not saying that no-one will wish to speak with you – far from. But it might make it that bit easier if you're already *used* to talking about how you feel and you're in the habit of doing so – it just makes it that bit less daunting. You know what I mean ;).

Remind People

Some of you may have people around you in the day during your Time Away from the Norm. Relish this! No matter how much they can get on your nerves at times – you are indeed very lucky! If you don't have anyone, this is fine, as there are many opportunities to have contact with people you know during the day – it really is a case of reminding people that you're around, and working out where they can fit you in (and vice-versa). For instance, it may be a case of speaking to a different friend each day whilst they munch on their Hula Hoops on their lunch break. Or maybe you know people that drive a lot for a living; perhaps delivering goods, through sales work or simply by driving from one client site to another – you could chat to them on the ol' hands-free (safety first!) whilst they drive. If people you know work from home sometimes – maybe they could come and do this round at yours one day, or you can pop to theirs, even if it's for just part of the day? Maybe someone you know has to travel by train to the other end of the country for a meeting or focus group. *Remind* them that you're available to talk and you can chat to them. This is also likely to be of benefit to the other person, as they are probably bored and may not have anyone else to chat to, in which case you have an all-round winner going on!

Going through your contacts list is also a great way to remind yourself of those around you. This may sound a bit basic, but I remember during my Time Away from the Norm there were other people that were in the same boat, but I'd completely forgotten about them. Your phone list and address book are fantastic places to start – really scrutinise each name as you scroll past them – you may also remember that they know someone who is currently having Time Away from the Norm and could really do with some companionship during their time off. You may come across a pregnant work colleague on maternity leave, a neighbour who's studying for their PhD, a friend who works flexi-time or even someone who's on annual leave and decided to stay put in the UK for a bit of downtime. There are more people out there having Time Away from the Norm than you realise, but it does take the time and effort to remember them. But once the hard work is over, you can really reap the rewards and enjoy having that bit of extra company around you :).

Lunch Meets a Treat!

Lunch is the one hour of the day when you know those around you can potentially be free, so why not meet your friends and family for lunch? 'Coz everyone's got to eat, right?!

Often people don't take a lunch break for whatever reason, but studies have proven that the benefits of having one are substantial – getting away from your desk, stretching your legs, inducing in a fresh supply of oxygen and actually enjoying the company of those you work with in a more relaxed and informal context – to name but a few. Most people actually know of these benefits – are fully aware of them in fact, but still for whatever reason decide that lunch behind their desk is far better than a mere ten-fifteen minute stroll and the benefits that this can bring. And don't even get me started with the hygiene factor of getting tuna and sweetcorn sandwich crumbs down the side of your keyboard(!). But this is where you, yes *you,* can become an ambassador and save those around you from being chained to their desks, and essentially save them from your own situation if you've been signed off work from stress and overworking.

Go visit those you know with a picnic to take to a green spot, check out a new bistro or simply grab a coffee – they're likely to be really happy and grateful that you've come to visit, and it's a great chance to catch-up with them. Plus with the way lunch breaks work, you can go and visit two people between the hours of 12pm and 2pm, if they work near one another. Maybe more – have a lunchtime marathon and see how many people you can squeeze in ;).

Although we've discussed the benefits to those around you by visiting them for lunch, do not forget the benefits this gives to *you*. Time Away from the Norm can be a lonely experience for some. Even if you feel that you have lots of people around you, you may feel isolated and alone at times due to your situation. An important thing to do is to maintain social contact with those around you, and as difficult as it may be at times, it's good to remain as open as possible regarding how you feel about things. A lunch break with someone you trust is a great way to do just this – even if you're feeling concerned about opening up, you know that there's a finite amount of time you'll be spending with them; normally an hour. So you know it will come to an end. Plus it gets you out and about – visiting different places, seeing new sights – it just helps break up the day that bit.

And if you're bored of your usual crowd, and are currently single, why not go on a lunch date?! Or if you're feeling really daring – just wander up to a stranger who takes your fancy on their lunch break and ask to join them! Many people do end up taking lunch breaks by themselves, sometimes to escape from their office and colleagues, but also because they don't really have anyone else to have lunch with. I've done this a couple of times, and found it to be quite amicable. The conversation is usually quite interesting and you never know where things may lead to... exciting stuff! Or you could just go meet your friends and family for lunch, that's also fine :).

Keep in Touch with Work Colleagues

This may not be beneficial in all cases, especially if your idea of a complete break from work doesn't involve seeing those you work with. But it is worth considering that the odd coffee or drink, and a bit of a catch-up with one or two trusted co-workers may be of benefit to you. As with anything, it will depend on your own circumstances and what you feel comfortable with, but sometimes when you are experiencing Time Away from the Norm, your workplace and working life may feel like a million miles away. And by seeing, or simply being in touch with a couple of frolleagues (friends at work!) could help you to maintain a sense of what's going on and help you feel less removed from your workplace. Plus, you get to catch-up on the latest gossip and happenings ;) – hey, it may make your own life feel like less of a drama!

If you feel up to it, (and I guess only if your company does this), you may fancy meeting your colleagues on special social occasions that have been organised. Maybe a small team affair is the most attractive option as a first visit – perhaps a lunch celebrating someone's engagement news or a leaving do. And once you've gotten used to this and feel that you could handle something bigger, if your workplace is having a bowling trip or a summer BBQ, perhaps you could attend this. Your colleagues are likely to be delighted to see you again, and it's a great way to meet up and chat in an informal environment and to keep those channels of communication alive.

Another great way of keeping in touch with your workplace is by getting your line manager or another trusted colleague to send you newsletters from your team or department – perhaps slides from a recent team or company meeting or perhaps just an email keeping you updated on any moves and changes that have taken place whilst you've been away. It could also include light-hearted news – anything from the sandwich man having a new jiggle and a wiggle to his step, to who won the Apprentice office sweepstake, or the all-important winner of the 'Marketing's Got Talent' contest. This could be quite a nice way to keep in touch with things, and so when you do return to work, you'll be so up-to-date, it won't feel like you've missed much at all, and you'll fit right back into the swing of things again :).

And if you've been made redundant, keeping in touch with old colleagues could also work in your favour from a networking point of view. It's tough, and again it may not be for everyone, but perhaps you can use a social meet as an occasion to find out about potential job vacancies, especially those that aren't officially advertised. Some of your former colleagues may know or encounter people looking for someone like you, and if you're around it's more likely to be your name that comes to mind, should the situation arise. Just something to think about, I guess.

Blind or otherwise – go on a Date!

When you're single, time flies and it's often the case that it's tricky to meet people – you're out working all day, then you see your friends, chat to your housemates, turn into Cinders and clean the house, blah blah, busy busy – and suddenly there's very little time left in the day. And after a full-on week you don't have the energy to muster batting your eyelashes, as you're struggling to keep them open from lack of sleep anyway! So perhaps your friends know of someone who's 'exactly your type.' Or just someone you never got round to asking out. Maybe see someone of the same gender as you. Go speed-dating. Whoever and whatever – now's the time! You'll end up meeting new people, going out to places you wouldn't normally go to – so what have you got to lose? On the other hand you may end up getting married, having kids and living happily ever after ;).

D-I-S-C-O

Yup, that's right – you certainly read that correctly, having a party of some type can be a really great way to get people together and to celebrate! OK, I know, you may not feel like you have much to celebrate. Life's pretty grim in fact. But hey, if you can think of five good things that you have in your life – perhaps the people in your life, your health, the fact that you have two legs to dance on, half-decent breath and an arm to hold your drink, then I think that that's reason enough to party! And if you do have limbs missing, then I'm damn well sure you can think of ten good things about your life. So have a party! A party can put you in good spirits and needn't be anything complicated. It can be as simple as inviting a bunch of mates round, blowing up a few balloons and sticking some music on. The rest will follow :).

People only tend to have a party when they feel they have something big and worthy to celebrate – their 40th Birthday (what about your 39th and 41st?!), when they move houses, their ruby anniversary, if they graduate etc etc. And although this is brilliant, and everyone should absolutely continue doing this – what about simply rejoicing in the fact that we're all alive, and that is reason enough to celebrate life? Keep on celebrating!

Maybe you're not comfortable having a party for yourself – why not throw one for someone you know? Perhaps your mate got divorced, your neighbour has a new job, your housemate got back from travelling, your brother wrote his car off and now has to catch the bus – throw them a party! You can also have a fancy dress theme – for our brother having to catch the bus example, maybe get everyone to dress up as different forms of public transport. Maybe have a London Underground theme where everyone picks a different Underground station to come dressed as. Just watch out for the one who turns up as 'Leytonstone' (late and stoned!). That or 'Cockfosters' on the Piccadilly line...! I bet your brother won't be feeling quite so down about writing his car off after such a party! And again it needn't be a party in the literal sense of the word – have a BBQ, a few drinks, a PJ and DVD night, tea and cake – in the words of Wayne's World – 'Party on Dude!'

Kids 'R' Us

OK, I don't have kids, so I may not know what I'm talking about here, but I feel that this is an important section to have. So <deep breath>, I'm going to give this my best shot: Your kids are your life and joy. You may not have enough time to spend with them as you're busy working, busy with this, busy with that, busy with life I guess. Well having Time Away from the Norm is the perfect chance for you to reclaim some quality time to invest back into these relationships again.

Even if your kids go to school, you can spend time and think of activities and things to do with them when they're not at school, including the weekend and evenings. So if it's an afternoon of wakeboarding, a spot of football at the park, a bowling trip at your nearest lanes, a long overdue shopping trip or some indoor skiing that you've been meaning to schedule in, then take up the opportunity to book this in now. And it needn't be big or expensive either – cinema on Wednesdays with 'Orange Wednesdays' (two for one cinema tickets), a nice picnic at the local park or simply a stroll around the countryside can work just fine – just something that gets you and your kids out and about, and allows you to spend that bit of time that your children love and crave. In fact, getting out and about walking in the country is a great habit to get into – the fresh country air, the scenic surroundings, the sights and sounds of nature – absolutely priceless.

And with your Time Away from the Norm, you can find out what works well for both yourself and your kids, and look to make this more of a regular occurrence for when you do return back to the working Norm. You'll be really grateful for your time away if it helps you to figure out and establish routines as important as spending time with your kids, and what works best for you all. Naturally, if you already do this with quite some ease – that's fantastic. But it doesn't hinder to have that spare bit of time to put in that extra bit of energy – as everyone likes to feel special and to know that that effort has been made for them. As that's human nature, after all ;).

And, OK, if you don't have any kids, you're not off the hook just yet! Now's a great opportunity to spend time with children you know, but don't really see much of. And the reason for this? Well, children just have this insatiable ability to cheer, energise and entertain, quite frankly. Not all, admittedly. But there's definitely something about the way children have little inhibitions – they will always say what they think; are curious, open-minded, inquisitive and just completely natural, I guess. And that's actually quite refreshing to be around and can give you a change in perspective, especially if you are normally only used to adult company. So whoever it is – your friends' kids, younger siblings or cousins – go pay them a visit!

Arena's Top-Tip Chapter Summary

✓ Head online and use the Gumtree website (and other local sites) to team you up with your local community and all its happenings

✓ Social networking has its caveats, but it's an undeniably great way to stay in touch and connected with others

✓ Picking up the phone is one of the best ways to get support during this time, regardless of how you may be feeling

✓ Remind friends and family that you may be around during the day, and are more than happy to have a catch-up and chin-wag with them

✓ Save those in your life from being chained to their desks and meet them for a combo of fresh air and Wotsits on their lunch break

✓ Keep in the loop with company news by staying in touch with a trusted work colleague or two

✓ Use your spare time to meet that someone special; plan that perfect date, spruce yourself up and woo them to pieces

✓ Celebrate each and every milestone – throw the simplest or zaniest of parties quicker than you can waltz out the YMCA

✓ Plan and spend time with your kids, and really relish the extra time you've been given to make this happen

4. Stretching Oneself!

Know your limits? No, we often don't until we're truly tried and tested. Now this chapter looks to test and expand your mind in ways that you may not be used to; in creative and fun ways that may be far from the working world Norm. It also looks to develop your skill-set and provide new stimulation whilst you're at it, so expect to discover some new hobbies, talents and interests along the way! Have fun testing and streeetching ;)!

Get a Hobby

You may be brimming with an assortment of hobbies, whether it's a bit of karate, playing basketball, collecting model cars, video editing or mixing cocktails. If you do, you'll understand the endless benefits of having one – how it enables you to have something of your own that you can enjoy, how it gives you a sense of satisfaction and personal accomplishment, and more significantly – it's something that provides you with a point of focus when the going gets tough. So, whatever your hobby may be, it's really worth valuing, nurturing and keeping a firm hold of.

If your hobbies have grown a bit sketchy over the years or work's taken over and you've forgotten what they were, then now's the ultimate time to pick this up and firmly reclaim it back in your life. Or maybe there's something that's always tickled your fancy and you want to give it a go. Whatever you fancy doing – learning to play the saxophone, a spot of juggling, some horse riding – find out about it and give it a go – who knows what doors it could open for you? Having a hobby is one of the key ways in enabling you to enjoy and make the most of your Time Away from the Norm, so even if you're someone who has hobbies ahoy, why not find an additional one to add to the collection? It can be as relaxing or as challenging as you'd like it to be.

Whatever you do, you'll probably find that you're an inspiration to those around you, and that you're doing something that others wish they could do if they had the time. I know I certainly had a lot of people telling me this during my Time Away from the Norm. Also there are people who work full-time, have spare time, yet don't have the courage or the drive to get a hobby, so here's where you can really stand out. Get you! So even though your hobby may not feel all too amazing at the moment, (or perhaps you've always had one, but just took it for granted) – this could be a fundamental part of your Time Away from the Norm, and you'll be thanking yourself before you know it. Honestly, I know I did ;).

Improve your Skill-Set

Now's a great time (as good as any!) to improve your skill-set more generally. If there are any gaps that you perceive, areas that you'd like to improve on, then now's a fab time to do just that! The Internet is a great place to get started to find out more information and to get inspired, but don't forget to look around and speak with people too, as these other avenues can prove to be just as effective, if not more so. But you know that already – you are smart and savvy ;).

So you may wish to learn to drive – and this is actually one of the best times you can do this. You can take lessons in the daytime instead of having to squeeze them in first thing in the morning before work or late in the evening. Learning to drive actually takes a lot more time than you realise – you need to learn the theory, learn the bonnet check and car maintenance questions and have the time to book in both your theory and practical tests. If you've never driven before or you're new to an area you'll need to spend time finding a suitable instructor – perhaps through the Yellow Pages, the Internet or a recommendation from someone you know. And then there's the matter of which car you wish to learn to drive in and whether it's an automatic or manual! Decisions, decisions :). Driving was something I did during my Time Away from the Norm, and I guess at the time it was a big deal to me; I'd get very nervous about my lessons (don't even get me started with how apprehensive I was about the test!), but in hindsight, I believe that it was actually very good for me. I only had one lesson a week, but with the work and preparation I was doing around each lesson, it really gave me something to focus on aside from my Time Away from the Norm – and it was something I really missed once I'd passed my test and it was all over. So even if it's something that's quite challenging and difficult, it really is worth doing. Not enough for me to want to take my test again though ;).

So driving was something that I did, but there really are scores of skills that you can gain and improve on during your Time Away from the Norm. So perhaps you'd like to improve your PC skills, so when you go back to the office, you'll be ahead of the game. Or perhaps you wish to learn some basic First Aid skills – think how priceless learning the very basics could be? Even if you just use them the once, how thankful would you be to have learnt such invaluable skills? Maybe you wish to learn counselling skills – there are so many different types out there, so if want to know your NLP from your CBT – get on the band wagon! And you don't have to become a counsellor to utilise these skills – you can use these on yourself, those around you, those you work with – anyone really. Maybe you wish to improve your ability to flirt, your DIY, tapestry, massage, horticulture, interior design, frame making or spider grooming skills... so many skills! You really can become a jack of all trades ;).

Reading & Writing

Now here's a game. How many books have you bought over the years, and not yet read? How many books have you said that you'll buy and not yet bought? How many books have you been recommended and you've said very adamantly that you'll read them, but not quite found the time to do so yet...?! OK, you catch my drift ;). Reading's a great way to pass the time and really helps escape to another level. So whether it's that travel guide on Latvia you've been meaning to look at, the latest detective novel in your favourite series, an autobiography of someone really awe-inspiring or simply a piece of easy-reading chick lit – dig out those reading glasses and discover the bookworm in you!

Reading can help you improve your work skills, develop a hobby, learn a new card trick, share an ancient recipe, teach you self-defence – literally whatever it is that floats your boat – there's sure to be a book on it. And even if you've never been an avid reader, I'm not talking big 1000-page novels here – you may just want to look through a magazine or comic, pick up a different daily newspaper to your usual, read that camera manual you've been meaning to look at or simply read that supplement that caught your eye, but you didn't quite get round to reading. It gets the mind thinking, pondering and questioning and ultimately keeps the curiosity firmly in drive. And again, when I say read, it doesn't have to be anything intense – you can skim, flick or just pick up the odd sentence here and there – this may be particularly useful if you're finding it difficult to concentrate on words at the moment. There really are no hard and fast rules about reading, so I would really recommend it.

And do not forget your local library. This is a great way to get out there and bring home those books that you wouldn't normally pick up – simply because they're free and hey, why not! Perhaps if you really get into reading during your Time Away from the Norm, you can even set up a reading club. This could be as simple as a group of friends meeting each month or so; taking it in turns to pick out a book and hosting an evening. Really simple, but really effective – it enables everyone to get together, share their views and discuss the book at hand, and just generally have some fun :). Try it.

And if you get bored of reading other people's work, why not write your own book? Many people are put off putting pen to paper and claim that they have to be some type of self-proclaimed author to do just that. Not true. You're reading this after all ;). There are many ways in which to get self-published, including launching your book online – Lulu (www.lulu.com) can help you do just that. If there's an idea you've always had, or you've picked up some inspiration from your latest trip away, or you started writing a book five years ago, but never really got round to completing it – then you should really give it a go! It could be a short story you'd like to write and share with a close network of friends and family, or perhaps it's a niche book aimed at a very specific audience. Alternatively, you may wish to make it big and have a bestseller ;). Whatever it is you'd like to write about, hidden talent or not, do give it a go – you never know what you'll be unleashing!

Do-You-Speak-Eng-lish...?

¡Hola! Dia duit! Laba diena! Wouldn't it be great to be able to say more than just 'hello' in another language? Wouldn't it be fab not to have to fly halfway round the world simply to ask the locals (veeery slowly!) if they speak English? Well guess what? Now's your chance to change that! If you've always fancied learning another language or you'd like to brush up on your language skills, learn a few sentences for your summer break in Italy or you're serious about becoming fluent in a range of languages – don't stop now! You may have taken French at GCSE, because you had to, but would now quite like to build on that foundation. Maybe you'd like to take advantage of some of the more topical languages, like Arabic, which could perhaps be useful to your career. Learn a language which has elaborate and beautiful symbols, like Japanese. Whichever you choose, and however many languages you wish to take on, the point is to keep it consistent and really give it a good stab!

You can learn a language in many different ways and the beauty of it is that it's really flexible and versatile, and you can absolutely go at your own pace. You can combine learning between books, CDs, online resources and attending actual classes. This will help you identify which way best suits you in terms of learning, and this can be more than one approach – a mixture of a few different methods even. Gumtree and other websites offer language swaps with other people, so this could also be a really great way for you to learn, as there's nothing quite like learning straight from a native speaker. And at the same time you get to put your teaching skills into practice by helping another person learn a language that you know. And don't worry if you don't know any other languages, as a lot of people simply wish to improve their English, especially if you're living in a city, where expatriates tend to congregate.

If you're still not convinced, and believe that you don't have a lingo bean within you, then a great way to overcome this is by getting a language buddy. This is someone else, a friend perhaps, that would also like to learn a language, and you both work together; helping and testing each other, and setting one another tasks and exercises to complete. This way, there's no getting away with it! But on a more serious note, it can really help act as a motivator as there's nothing more encouraging than someone else attempting the same thing as you, especially with the more competitive amongst us! So start picking out that new language buddy of yours ;). And perhaps as a treat, when you both learn the basics, you could go on a holiday to a country which speaks the language you've been learning. So you'd better start getting that Greek to a half decent level if you fancy hopping between the beautiful islands of Kimolos and Kythnos! And don't stop at a language buddy – if there are a few of you that would like to learn a language, then you could even start up your own language club! Think about it...

Get Snap Happy!

Simple, easy and versatile, photography is a great hobby to take up. Most people will have a camera of some kind, or have one that they can borrow or have access to from someone – you can use anything from a £5.99 Boots disposable, a digital compact to a high-tech DSLR. And it doesn't matter how amateur you are – absolutely anyone can have a go, and with the majority of cameras being digital these days, you can take as many pictures as you like and view them before selecting and printing them. Genius! This may not seem like a big deal to you, but believe me, in a recent photography class I enrolled on where people were considerably older, this was a *very* big deal – my course mates had spent their lifetimes developing films and still find digital to be a bit of a novelty. I guess it's good to be reminded of the days when you didn't have the luxury of selecting and deleting the worst of the crop.

Anyhow, a camera gets you out and about. You can plan day trips to locations around where you live – a local park, your town centre or simply ambling around and generally photographing people, action or nature. The location can be as simple as you like – you can spend hours photographing your local surroundings, or it could be adventurous – perhaps travelling to scenic spots of interest, green belt areas, special monuments, heritage sites – whatever takes your fancy and interest really. Or why not become a tourist for the day and tie in your photography with a bit of sight-seeing – you know you've always wanted to take an open bus tour really...! Maybe even combine it with a bit of walking – there's nothing quite like seeing a place on foot and capturing those moments naturally.

As you get into it and wish to challenge yourself further, you can set yourself special projects that you wish to base your work around, for instance moving water, action sports or people portraits. You could also create a portfolio of your work and even look to get it published. The trick in this is concentrating on one area – and the best way to do this is by looking at the pictures you would normally take, and thinking about the target audience for these photos. This way, you can make a list of publications of your focus audience, establish a contact there and send a couple of your shots across. Although you may not make any money from it, it would be great to get your picture in a specialist magazine, plus there may be a non-financial reward available for it – I know someone who bagged a free all expenses paid holiday from a cutting-edge shot he took one morning! Not bad, eh?! And if nothing comes about from it, at least you've had the chance to try something you wouldn't normally have done. And that's always a winner, right?

Another tip is to 'Think Local.' Sometimes just getting down to local events that are taking place in your area is a great way to get your work published, as well as enabling you to get to know your community that bit better. Often the local photographer has had a snooze too many, turned up late or simply hasn't captured all that's going on at the event. This is where your shots can help complete the picture. Quite literally. Imagine getting some of your work published – what an amazing thing to achieve during your Time Away from the Norm!

Blog it

Blogging's all the rage these days. And it's really straight-forward and easy too. Think of a topic, any topic; a hobby, an experience, an idea or perhaps just writing about your Time Away from the Norm! Now this is a *great* idea – who wouldn't wish to know about your time off – the fact that you're doing something interesting and different each day when everyone else is doing the <yawn> monotonous? If anything, it will probably motivate you to have something in your diary on a regular basis, not only for your own experience and enjoyment, but to also write about and share with others. It's also quite a nice way to let others know what you've been up to and to keep them posted. And it doesn't have to be all fun and games either. Sometimes Time Away from the Norm can be incredibly challenging and it's good to have an outlet for this. As with the journal and diary writing mentioned earlier on (chapter 2), writing can be an excellent way for you to express yourself and channel your emotions and any difficulties you've been encountering. You'll also be surprised to realise that there are others out there who feel the same. I didn't do this when I had my Time Away from the Norm, but absolutely think that you should give it a go! If, of course, you'd like to write about a hobby you have, then this is absolutely fine too. You can write, rant, shout, roar... whatever you like – blogging really is what the cool kids do ;).

Give your Brain a Workout!

Exercising your brain is *so* underrated! 'Wait a minute... it'll come to me in a second... I'm sure it will, hold on a mo...' Sound familiar? Yup, we moan all the time when we can't remember things clearly, be it someone's name, the way to Scunthorpe or what you had for breakfast this morning. And then there's not being able to calculate things as quickly as you Once Upon a Time could. Well change that! Today :). It can be really fun too, and you can add it into your daily routine quite easily. Perhaps you can do the crossword in the daily newspaper, find a different way of solving a problem, try out a Sudoku puzzle, do some creative thinking, take a new route to somewhere familiar or puzzle yourself in a word tease. Look around for something that gets you thinking; be it with words or numbers or otherwise – you choose. Do take your time to find something you enjoy and that ultimately challenges you – it is your brain after all, so fully worth the investment of time. Maybe even supplement this with finding out about pub quizzes in your local area and getting a team of you together to attend each week. You never know, you and your friends might have a real knack for them (just make sure you have a mate who knows about *the* most bizarre stuff!) and can win some great prizes too – I remember some friends winning a Nintendo Wii once. Not bad for a Thursday night in the local!

You can be really interactive about this too. Brain workouts on the Nintendo DS are a great way to do this on the go, as well as other computer programmes and games on the Internet. Nothing like giving the brain a good workout! And although it doesn't happen overnight, exercising your brain really does get your mind thinking quicker, working sharper and generally gives you a great confidence boost. And don't dismiss quiz shows either, especially if you have Challenge TV! There are shows on all the time, so you can take your pick from Bob Holness (remember Blockbusters?!), Carol Vorderman or Anne Robinson – whoever does it for you really. And you can pick game shows depending on the level of difficulty you require (and build yourself up), or perhaps choose a show based on a subject of interest that you have or an area that you'd love to be smart at (c'mon, everyone has a subject area like that!). And do not fret if you don't have Challenge TV, as there really are many shows on every channel focusing on general knowledge. In fact, why not team your favourite show with a pot of brew in the afternoon? Relaxation, a cup of tea and bigger brain cells all at the same time. Now *that's* brain power ;).

Arena's Top-Tip Chapter Summary

- ✓ Now is the time to reclaim or develop a new hobby to give you a brand new sense of focus and enjoyment
- ✓ Examine your skill-set and look to use your time off to fill in any gaps that you have – for pleasure or future gains; you can never have too many skills under your belt
- ✓ Dig out those reading glasses and catch-up on all those books you've been missing out on (with tea and chocolate HobNobs, granted!)
- ✓ Give your lingo skills a good twizzle by learning a language – something you already have the basics for or something nouveau
- ✓ The simplest of hobbies: grab a camera and step out to your natural surroundings to capture that moment
- ✓ Blogging gets your creative skills in motion, so take a trip to cyberspace and get your thoughts, POV and opinions right out there
- ✓ Give that grey matter of yours a great big stir by doing some kind of brain workout – it can do no wrong and will get the mind thinking in more ways than usual

5. Looking After Numero Uno!

Looking after number one is important at all times. We all know that. But sometimes we end up forgetting this and neglecting ourselves, for whatever reason. Not now though; now is the time when looking after yourself could not be more fundamental. You may be feeling a whole kettle of mixed emotions at the moment, and this may be deterring you from the very basics of taking care and looking after yourself properly. Well, this chapter is about to sort that right out! It covers the core essentials – and once you keep these at a constant, you'll find it easier to work on other things once you have this foundation laid. Now, let's crack on!

Me, Myself & I

A self-MOT is something that we sometimes neglect, as we often take our bodies for granted. We think we'll be fit and healthy forever; "nothing's going to happen to me" you say. Or you just forget. Simple as. Well you won't be thinking that when you're 75 with rotting, false teeth and toe nails that are so far in-grown that there's no saving them... now there's a thought and a half!

When was the last time you had a dental check-up? Your ears checked? A smear test (female over 25s only), your blood pressure, diabetes and cholesterol levels checked? Are you up-to-date on all your boosters and jabs? Are you going on holiday soon and need to sort out some immunisations? That's quite a lot already, and obviously your own checks will be different depending on your gender, age and family history. So it's really worth using your Time Away from the Norm to get on top of these and maybe peg-mark future appointments in your diary (electronically or on paper), so that you never miss them again. Perhaps ensure that you get sent a reminder letter, email or text nearer the time. Another good idea is to keep a note of all your stats in one place, so you can easily refer to them when needed. Explore the options and see what works best for you so you can set this up for the future and never miss that all important check-up or screening.

Perhaps you fancy a bit of a change. Why not? Maybe you've always wanted to try contact lenses, but never really had the patience for them, or the thought of putting something in your eyes makes you want to jump out the nearest window. It's worth exploring options, as lenses have become considerably more comfortable, and with practise can be quite straight-forward. I was someone who was mortified at putting contacts (or anything for that matter!) in my eyes, but was then taught to aim for the 'whites' of my eyes. This helped considerably and with my Time Away from the Norm, I was able to take the time to learn to do this and am now a contact lens advocate :). And with free trials widely offered and cheap contacts available online, it's dead easy. Perhaps you wish to take it one step further and look to get laser eye surgery. *Imagine* waking up and not stumbling around for your glasses each day or having to take your contacts out when you wish to have that cheeky afternoon kip?! Again, free consultations are available, so you really do have nothing to lose!

Maybe your body just needs a bit of a break and the number one thing for rejuvenating it can be a spa break away. And these really don't have to be uber expensive – www.lastminute.com frequently have their £10 sales, and with your Time Away from the Norm, you have no excuse for not getting yourself ready in front of your laptop (tea in hand!) before the sale commences. You can maybe do a spa break with a family member, friend or perhaps by yourself – whatever you fancy. Or maybe just have a one-off facial, massage or go sit in the sauna or jacuzzi at your local pool. And it's quite a nice habit to get into. I remember someone who regularly booked herself in for spa treats every couple of months, and never quite got why she was 'wasting' her annual leave on this at the time. But now I get that she simply took her R&R (rest and relaxation) very seriously (I salute her!), and that it's an essential thing to remember to do. And to keep on doing.

And these really are just a few ideas to get you thinking, as there are many different ways to look out for number one and to achieve this. But whatever you end up doing – just remember to take the time to look after yourself – those teeth aren't going to take care of themselves, after all ;).

Up the Nutrition

Not my expert arena here, but even I know the difference in how I feel when I've been splurging out on cherry cola and Haribo all morning, and then indulging on a greasy pile of fish and chips and cake for lunch, and wondering why I feel so cranky, bloated and dehydrated – far quicker than I can say lardalicious. This versus something like a healthy combo of fresh fruit and veg, a mix of different food groups and some good ol' trusty H2O. You know how eating well can have an impact on your mood and just generally in how you feel. So if you're not feeling tip-top mood wise, then doing something you can control by eating healthily really does make a great deal of sense. Plus, you're smart – you don't need me to go into the benefits of how eating healthily helps keep the digestive system healthy, your immune system intact and protects you against all those serious diseases out there.

And if you're not too down with your carbs and your iron levels, the key to a healthy balanced diet is to eat a *variety* of foods –

this ensures that you get all the vitamins, minerals, protein and other ingredients you need to be healthy, each day. A few simple rules to follow are to have at least five portions of different fruit and veg every day and a range of the various food groups – a bit of starch in wholegrain foods such as bread, pasta, rice and cereals, servings of dairy (including low-fat milk) and some protein-rich foods such as lean meat, fish, eggs, poultry, beans and lentils. It should also be low in fat, especially saturated fat, and salt and sugar intake ought to be kept at a minimal – try using spices and herbs to flavour instead, as well as fruit to curb the sweet tooth, if you have one. I know I do ;).

And with all this talk of food – don't forget to do just that – to eat! And although this may sound really pretty obvious, it is something that is easily forgotten when you have other things on your mind. Or you may just not feel particularly hungry or perhaps you're eating more than usual – simply because you're bored, and quite frankly it tastes damn good. The key here, and throughout this guide, is to create your own Norm; your own routine unique to *you* – so ensure that you have three main, good, hearty meals a day. Maybe they're slightly smaller portions than usual, as you're not using your usual level of energy. That's fine. But the trick is to keep it regular and not to neglect it – skipping meals is a real no-no!

Get the Blood Pumping!

As evil, spine-chilling and shuddering as the word 'exercise' may sound, it really does work in helping you feel tip-top. *Really.* Now I used to be very guilty of not doing enough (or any!) exercise at times, but now have my exercise routine firmly implanted in me, and wouldn't choose to have it any other way. And that's really saying something coming from someone who used to do next to zilch! I've come a long way, baby :).

And it needn't be difficult! So it's the middle of winter and the thought of venturing out to the frost and minus something temperatures isn't too appealing, or perhaps your fitness levels are a little worse for wear – then let TV aerobics be the answer! Please note that there are other exercise channels available for the more hard-core amongst us, although TV aerobics is highly applicable to virtually anyone – the exercises are by no means easy, and will certainly stir up the grey matter and get you concentrating and co-ordinating quicker than you can say Mr Motivator! (Remember him?!). These channels can be a real confidence booster before you try out at the gym, and include everything from weight lifting to step, as well as chair aerobics for the elderly (or the amateurs amongst us). They're filled with their own health and safety warnings, so I shan't bore you with those, although I would hasten to add that it really is worth checking that you do have lots of space around you – nothing like knocking that eight foot plant or full length lamp over... ahem!

You can also make your own exercise routine or circuits – a few sit-ups, running up and the down the stairs or some weight lifting – those one litre mineral water bottles (or baked beans cans for beginners!) really do get the muscles going! For those of you seriously looking to take up exercising at home (I salute you!), it may be worth investing in some dumbbells, a stepper or even something as simple as a hula hoop. Happy toning! And for the more interactive amongst us, games consoles like the Wii fit are also great ways to get fit, and with their array of games and goal-setting approaches to weight control (if that's your aim), it can set you in the right direction towards your fitness goal. Plus you'll have lots of spare time to get the top scores on all the games ;).

Obviously nothing substitutes getting out there and doing some sport, whether this is in a playing field, at a gym or by simply going for a run, jog or walk. You may find your local leisure centre has various exercise classes and sport societies available, or you may wish to try out a new sport that you've been meaning to have a go at – so if fencing, climbing, golf or jujitsu takes your fancy, then *do* give it a go! And don't forget that it's not just local leisure centres and gyms that have the answer; universities and independent sporting groups are also great places to check out, and may have something of interest for you. And keep your eyes peeled (and other people's!) in the local papers, ads online, libraries or lampposts (just a few examples!) for that quirky new sport to try out.

R&R Time

A bit of rest and relaxation never did anyone any harm. And this feeds on nicely from the previous section on exercise, as although this is linked, it offers a slightly less adrenaline pumping alternative. If you've been signed off work for stress or anxiety, then this can really help you. Relaxation is something that as an adult tends not to come as naturally to us as it perhaps did when we were young kids. And through learning these basic skills in relaxation we can help improve our wellbeing and utilise them at any stage of our lives, as well as educating those around us of them. Which I can assure you will have to do when everyone asks you what the secret to that special relaxed glow in you is ;).

Relaxation can take a variety of different forms and can include anything from tai chi, yoga, meditation, walking, fishing, cycling, golf, playing an instrument – or even just practising and concentrating on breathing deeply to help you relax. It certainly can take a range of forms, and it's really up to you to try some different ones out and figure out which works best for you. It's also important to note that if one class or instructor doesn't work out, you shouldn't write it off just yet. In most instances the subject is very big and has different areas of focus. So for example if one type of meditation doesn't suit you, it's worth trying another one out. Meditation in fact is actually a big area – there are many different types – ones that concentrate simply on breathing (which comes from the belief that this is the one thing we have with us from the moment we are born until we die), to sitting in silence for five days (Vipassana meditation), to those that involve a bit more yoga and stretching. Either way, you need to discover the one right for you. It's also worth exploring the regulatory body online to investigate your options, or speaking with experts in the field and those around you for their experiences, advice and recommendations. Maybe you're already familiar with one or more of these relaxation techniques. If that's the case, now might be the time to increase the amount you do or to maybe try an alternative to team with what you're already doing. You're doing good :).

If you're struggling to relax or are finding yourself tenser than usual, try some basic techniques that you can easily implement into your daily life to help you relax: take a long hot bath, put some freshly scented flowers in the main room that you use, use fragranced relaxing candles, aromatherapy oils and calming CDs – whichever ticks your boxes. The more open you are to trying different techniques and ideas, the more likely you are to find the best mix for you or to stumble upon something completely new and different that truly works a treat. So do keep an open mind and don't close any doors before you've given them a go. And as usual, this applies to every aspect in dealing with Time Away from the Norm in helping you get the most out of your situation.

The Wacky Backy & all its Friends

The most serious in this chapter; cigarettes, alcohol and drugs are what I'm talking about here. The temptation may be there to bake some hash brownies and have a giggle too many. Or to make a concoction of all the drinks around you and get steamingly battered. Even to smoke that pack of twenty simply because you can, and hey why not. But it just isn't the answer. And when you are feeling a whole pick 'n' mix of emotions, it's really easy to do just that. But it *really* doesn't help in the long run. It may feel amazingly fantastic at the time, it really will, and it may feel great for as long as you carry on doing this. But sooner or later the novelty will wear off – sometimes sooner than you'd like it to. And you won't just be left with a splitting headache, the inability to pick your head up off the pillow and your breath smelling like an ashtray (yeouch!). At the time you may have said and done some things that you now regret when you were in this state, and although people are likely to be sympathetic, it doesn't really help to push those around you away from you – you need them to be on your side to support you. And there's always the scenario that they're not sympathetic; it is self-inflicted after all, and another problem on your hands is not what you need right now.

And I don't want you to think I'm going all Yank on you, but there is that whole health and safety element to it when you're seemingly trollied and your judgement is slightly impaired; you can trip, fall and really cause yourself some serious injury. Not great if you're home alone and there's no-one due back for a few hours. Plus the wacky backy and its friends are highly addictive. And I know you know what that means. You may have experienced it first-hand or seen the effects of it on those close to you or through someone you know. It's not pleasant. And yes I know how Time Away from the Norm can be really challenging and boring – all those empty pockets of time. Perhaps it wasn't even your choice to be off work and you feel sorry for yourself, and are now you're taking it out on yourself. I understand that. But this really isn't the most productive way to fill time. The best way is to keep these temptations at bay and to seriously look at other ways to help yourself – there's plenty of other ways out there, and again – you *know* there are. So come back from the clouds, and continue reading this guide for some grounded ideas to help you on your way.

Those Purse Strings

Just keep an eye on them. You may find that having Time Away from the Norm means that you generally end up spending more money than you would normally tend to. When you're at work, unless you're an eager beaver online shopper (I've sat next to a couple of avid shoppers in my time!), you're likely just to buy your lunch and the odd pint after work. OK, you may do the occasional thing in the evening, but on the whole, your working day really is just that: working. But with Time Away from the Norm, you may end up being out and about a fair bit, which is great, but you may also spend money a lot more readily than you usually would.

A good way to combat this is by doing a simple budget – work out what you have, take away the essentials that you have to put aside (mortgage, bills, insurance, travel, food, savings and whatnot), and then divide this by four. As with all of the examples in this guide, this can be as simple or as complex as you like (a big fancy spreadsheet or a quick sum on a piece of scrap paper). The main point is to ensure that you're on top of your finances and that you don't create financial issues for yourself whilst off work. The next page shows an example of a monthly budget sheet you can use – just to give you an idea and a template to work with. Happy budgeting!

INCOME	Projected Amount	Actual Amount	Difference
Salary			
Any Other Income			
Income Subtotal			
HOME EXPENSES	Projected Amount	Actual Amount	Difference
Mortgage/Rent			
Bills			
Internet/Cable/Satellite			
Food			
General Maintenance			
Home Expenses Subtotal			
DAILY LIVING	Projected Amount	Actual Amount	Difference
Eating Out/Lunches/Snacks			
Drinking/Going Out			
Gym Membership			
Mobile Phone Bill			
Transport			
Holidays			
Hobbies			
Presents/Donations			
Other			
Daily Living Subtotal			
DEBT PAYMENTS	Projected Amount	Actual Amount	Difference
Credit Cards			
Student Loans			
Other Loans			
Debt Payments Subtotal			
MONTHLY BUDGET SUMMARY	Projected Amount	Actual Amount	Difference
Total Income			
Total Expenses			
NET			

Treat Time!

Now I'm not saying indulge yourself with a ten scoop knickerbockerglory with chocolate sauce drizzled all over with sprinkles ahoy (yum!). But what I am talking about here is something that you perceive to be as a bit of a treat, and rewarding yourself with this from time to time with the good work that you've been doing and your achievements so far. So stop, take a deep breath and reward yourself :). Having Time Away from the Norm is by no means easy and you shouldn't be too hard on yourself if you are struggling with it and finding it difficult at times. So to help, identify something that you see as a treat, something small, something special, and enjoy it :). Sometimes just verbally thanking or congratulating yourself for achieving a goal or milestone is also enough. Well done you!

Keeping it in Balance

I appreciate that this guide, teamed with some of your own ideas, as well as ideas from those around you may be a lot to take in at times. A little overwhelming even. It may have made you think about things you previously hadn't thought of doing or had perhaps overlooked. Maybe it has helped you open your eyes up to some of the possibilities of what you can achieve whilst you're off work. If so, that's super :). But what's important to ensure is that you don't overload yourself, as this is something that can happen very easily. So if you've picked a few things that you'd like to try out, then that really is fantastic – just don't try to do it *all.* You know your own limits – you know what you can handle, so I'm not going to give you figures and guidance as to how much or how little you should be doing. Plus we're all different, after all. If you're not sure yourself, which is *completely* normal by the way, (who's going to know in advance how much calligraphy, ceramics, dog walking and learning to flirt is appropriate for an average week?!), then one of the best ways to realise this is by constantly checking and asking yourself if you're doing the right amount or whether you need to slow down, take a break or alternatively up the ante. So questions like 'is this too much for me?', 'does this feel alright?', 'is this stressing me out a bit?' or 'could I be making this a tad more challenging?' are all fine to ask. You can make up your own questions, and you'll know the reason why you are signed off work, so you can ask yourself the most appropriate questions. You can do this each day, week or even spontaneously – however often you feel that you need it and to whatever degree you feel most comfortable with. And not only will such questioning keep you in good habits for staying attuned to your own feelings and how you are doing, but it will also ensure that you're concentrating on the *present* and that you've got the right amount of stuff going on for you *now*, as feelings originate in the moment.

And you don't have to think about how you feel on a really deep level – simply acknowledging your feelings and what they mean to you is enough. Plus, remember – there is no 'right' or 'wrong' in terms of your feelings – in fact, they are always right, as they are what you are feeling. If you can master this skill, it will serve you well for life. Because how often have you rushed through your 101 tasks a day, yet not given much thought as to whether you're doing what you wish to be doing or not? These questions are great as they then get you used to asking follow-up questions, such as 'can I give this to someone else to do?', 'can I leave this for another day?', 'what am I getting in return for what I'm doing right now?' These types of questions will ensure that your focus and goals are exactly where you want them to be, as by constantly checking and directly addressing them helps check that you are going in the right direction.

The Importance of Being Idle

Not just a great Oasis track, 'just being' is a really fundamental concept, and again, one that very easily gets overlooked. Have a go. Sit there: Ponder. Wonder. Daydream. Mooch. Mong out. Whatever you call it, it's worth doing from time to time, as not doing anything is often considered something of a luxury. And don't punish yourself for this; if you're someone who normally works really hard and likes to keep going and going, but sometimes you 'just don't feel like it' – that's fine – you are human, and as a human being you are designed to be fallible and you can *just be!* Everyone needs a bit of 'me' time :). And it's sometimes nice just to sit, listen to the sounds around us, notice how we feel, absorb our surroundings and genuinely relish our senses. Try it:

take a break, look up and relax... You'll also be surprised at how much you notice when you simply stop, do nothing and really take note. Another great time to do this is when you have your headphones on loud and the music's pumping – perhaps you're out on a walk – take your headphones out at certain intervals and absorb the sounds. You may find that the noises around you become amplified and you notice the smallest of sounds from the birds in the background, the rustling of leaves and the wind in the air. Nice. Another great trick is to pay particular attention to one sense over another, but in a deliberate manner – so focus on the smells around you, and then the sounds – take note of what you observe. Small pockets of time to be idle really reconnect you with your senses and your surroundings, which at other times simply go unnoticed. Definitely give it a go. And listen to the track as well – it's a cracker!

Get your Full 40 Winks in!

Ah, a blissful night's sleep. Heaven. Nothing quite beats it really, and it's completely underrated what a good night's sleep can do to you – it replenishes, revitalises and repairs, as well as helping to keep our minds and bodies healthy. Now for most, sleep is something you don't have to think about; it's an automatic process that occurs at the end of the day – bingo, you switch off to the land of nod. However, whilst experiencing Time Away from the Norm, sleep may become something of a struggle, what with a million and one thoughts spinning around in your mind, and whatnot. You may have trouble getting to sleep, and once asleep – managing to stay asleep. Now everyone has their own version of tips on how to get to sleep, and you may have your own too. If you don't – Google it – there's *plenty* out there ;). Here are a handful of some of my ideas: having a hot shower / bath, listening to a calming CD, using candles and oils, avoiding heavy meals too late, exercising (but not too late in the evening as this produces adrenaline), avoiding caffeine after a certain point in the day (I have a 5pm watershed!), writing down your troubles and woes before you go to sleep... to name but a few!

The key with having a range of sleeping techniques is to try different ones out and then noting the ones that work best for you.

Establishing those that are most effective and those that are less so enable you to create a type of chart or ranking to use depending on how much trouble you are having sleeping. So if you're having a slight bit of difficulty getting to sleep, and just need that boost to send you on your way, then maybe using a technique further down your list will nicely do the trick. The point is to take note of what works best for you, and to focus on this along with the other elements in this chapter of taking care of yourself (they all go hand-in-hand), which will enable you to build a sound strategy to a good night's sleep. And after experiencing a period of insomnia, a good night's sleep really is true bliss :).

Minimise the Gloom – Think Upbeat!

As clichéd as it may sound, a positive outlook never hurt anybody. This may seem a challenge when experiencing Time Away from the Norm, when naturally your Mojo may not be in ship-shape condition and wishes nothing but to sink. That's fine and understandable. But there's no harm in attempting to lift your mood, especially as emotions contribute so significantly to our energy levels and impact heavily upon our thinking and decision-making ability. And this doesn't have to be full-on beaming, big smiles and forced laughter at every opportunity – it can be as small as you like. Perhaps see if you can change your typical perception on things – so instead of 'I f*&king hate that rug – it is so bright and garish, only a lunatic would keep such a thing!' (ouch – that's a harsh one – notice insult to both rug *and* self). Well this could be transformed to 'wow, I love my rug – it's so original and bright – it's a one of a kind and totally reflects its owner: me!' Now that's much better :). See how many times you can do this in a day – almost as a challenge to yourself. This is also known as an element of Cognitive Behavioural Therapy, which if you hold your horses, I will touch on again in 'Self-help' (chapter 11).

A key point to remember here is that you always have a *choice* in how you react to most everyday scenarios – so it *is* within your control. And if the voice in your head is telling you that it's not possible and doing a good job of convincing you that it'll never happen – then tell it otherwise. And tell it in a *far* louder voice! Listen to the roar of positivity coming from within instead!

And there really are many ways to act in a more uplifting manner. Perhaps go on a negativity detox – see if you can go the week without saying something negative about a person, item, place or event. Much harder than it sounds! Find five strangers a day to smile at. Not in some freakish, outlandish way that initiates a swift phone call to security – just a natural, genuine smile. Smiling is infectious after all :). And if this still sounds like way too much hard work, then maybe note the personal benefits to yourself that acting in a more positive light could bring to you whilst experiencing Time Away from the Norm. And yes, it can be really hard to have a positive outlook when things feel like they're falling apart – but hey, the benefits can truly outweigh the effort. And I believe an upbeat approach is far more likely to be remembered than a gloomy outlook, and this may open doors and work wonders for you. And another thing: remember, negative thoughts produce and enhance stress hormones, which is a real no-no for whatever reason you've been signed off work for. And you know that.

Now you may already have your own positivity inducing methods. I know someone who hangs up positive phrases around his bedroom and reads them regularly, almost like a mantra. It works really well for him, as he begins to believe in them and reads them in a strong, bold voice which then has a positive impact on his outlook and behaviour. And don't forget, you don't have to have deeply profound words or sayings – I remember reading the chorus of Chumbawamba's 'I get knocked down' (Tubthumping) on someone's wall once and it apparently worked a treat for them! Have a stab. Once you identify and list how it can affect you in a positive way, you may feel more encouraged to make that extra ounce of effort. And again, the more you do it – the easier it genuinely gets. I guess you just become comfortable with being uncomfortable. I never used to believe that rule, but now swear by it, as I've seen how it can make such a notable difference. So if I do harp on about it a lot, you'll know why ;).

Another key when experiencing Time Away from the Norm is not to focus and compare yourself with others. I know this is human nature, and we all do it at some stage or another. But now is not the time. This is *your* time off, and if you're not doing so great, then wasting energy focusing on others, when you barely have enough going for yourself really isn't the way forward. Instead, focus all your efforts on you and what you can do for yourself – *now's* the time for this. That can also mean avoiding Facebook, as let's face it – we only go on it to rant about the utmost glory and happy days of our lives and to announce the fab, funny and fantastic. And we're all clever enough to know that that's not an everyday occurrence. And if you really have to think of others – just think of everyone bored at work with their deteriorating postures, dehydrated skin, going cross-eyed whilst staring simultaneously at the computer screen and the clock standing still at 9.03am... ;). And if you still need that boost – get out your 'Inspiration' book and pay *great* attention to it!

Arena's Top-Tip Chapter Summary

- ✓ Don't take your body for granted – remember to go for all those check-ups that may recently have gone unchecked
- ✓ Remember: three (good) meals a day, five portions of fruit and veg and a balance of different food groups – you know the drill!
- ✓ Friend or foe: exercise can really help you reap ample benefits to your mood, health and energy levels
- ✓ Fit in some R&R time – it is what the doctor ordered after all, and can be achieved in more ways than slouching about on that beanbag of yours
- ✓ The impact of increasing your intake of drugs, alcohol and cigarettes is a big no-no – feeling on top of the world (under the influence) sadly won't last forever
- ✓ If you're not accustomed to working out a budget on a regular basis, now's a great time to do this when your routine is out of sync from the working Norm
- ✓ Give yourself a break and a treat from time to time – you deserve it to celebrate the milestones you're been achieving
- ✓ Keep tabs on yourself by checking that you have your balance intact – that you are going out there and giving things a go, but not overloading yourself at the same time
- ✓ From time to time – simply stop, take a break, look up and relax – just be
- ✓ Note and rank your top sleeping tips and put your techniques into practice for a good night's sleep
- ✓ Get your positive thinking into first gear and challenge your mind when it wants nothing but to self-destruct and send out the negative

6. Home Is Where The Heart Is

Whether it's a caravan, semi, bungalow or penthouse – your home is your base, and fundamentally where you'll end up spending a lot of your Time Away from the Norm. There are plenty of things that you can do around and about the home, and the following pages show just a selection of what can be done. So dig out that 'to-do' list and get your pen poised at the ready!

Keep the Mice at Bay(!)

Now cleaning really isn't my thing. And I imagine if you're anything like me, then it's not exactly your idea of fun either. However, it really is worth considering the effect it can have on your body versus lounging about on the sofa and doing next to zilch. Moving and cleaning will not only have a positive impact on your immediate living environment, but it really does raise your energy levels and make you feel that bit better. I remember the wooden floor in our living room was becoming increasingly sticky after one house party too many and decided to clean it. I found some things under the sofa that I would much rather have found sooner than later(!) – but not only this, it made me feel a lot more positive and fuelled with energy, and hence made it easier for me to then get up and do other things. More fun things, I guess. And I kind of enjoyed it in the end anyway, singing along to 'The Time Warp' at the top of my voice ;). Plus, cleaning will win you some brownie points with those you live with – bonus!

And if you don't like the idea of 'cleaning' per se, then perhaps the title of a 'spring clean' has better connotations for you. Everyone has clutter (and if you don't, I am highly envious!), things you don't need any more, things that no longer fit you, things that you're bored of, things that don't belong to you(!) – to mention but a few. Now is the time to take charge and clear out that over-filled closet once and for all!

And don't forget the attic! Now this is a whole new territory we're exploring here – when was the last time you checked out your attic? Old school books from when you were ten, ancient photo albums, suitcases of trash... it's all happening up there – take a look. And who knows, not only will you feel super fantastic and uber organised for sorting out your stuff, you may find things that you can sell, give to charity or even pass onto others. So you really will be spreading the spring cleaning love :).

Sort out the Mundane

<Yawn>. Yep, the mundane often does send a yawn and the eyelids pointing southwards. But stifle that yawn, and crack right on with it, I

say! There's nothing quite like sorting things out and ticking items off a 'to-do' list. You know the feeling! And sorting out the mundane is often something that doesn't take very long in reality, once you make that kick-start. So if it's bills and insurance and letters in general that need filing – put on that energy-boosting CD and graft away! And whilst you're at it, it's good to set up Direct Debits and online billing systems – saves space on shelves, helps preserve the planet's resources, as well as saving you the odd bob for making it easier for the company at hand by using a paperless approach.

Another tip is to take the time to find better deals on products you're paying for, so whether this is car insurance, healthcare bills or heating and electricity products – there's normally always a cheaper option. Often there's an alternative that you hadn't previously considered – a better package that suits your needs, a new option that has become available, or perhaps your household spending has changed and you need a more suited product. Maybe you bought a package in a hurry with every good intention of changing it to a more appropriate one once you had the time, but didn't quite get round to it... Sound familiar? Anyway, whatever your reason, now's a greater time than any to find that better deal, and potentially end up saving a considerable amount of money. After all, who wants to spend more money than they need to on something like *insurance...?!*

Whilst sorting out that cheaper insurance for your beloved hamster, it's also worth checking your financial bank accounts – do you have the best bank account for all your monetary habits? Now, even if you're clued up and know your ISAs from your TESSAs (check you out!), it's well worth booking an appointment at your local bank branch for some simple, impartial advice. Many people don't utilise this free service that is available as part of having a bank account and are really missing out. These trained advisors can advise you on your personal financial needs, ensure that you're getting the best from your bank and money, and just generally help you out. They may even offer you a cup of tea! Now, who would turn such a fine offer down?

And there really is always 'stuff' that needs doing. Big stuff, small stuff, medium sized stuff – it all needs doing! Perhaps you have some clutter lying around or maybe after the spring clean you did, you collated many items you'd now like to rid yourself of. You could eBay these items and earn that bit of extra cash from them at the same time.

When was the last time you cleaned the car? Like properly cleaned it – vacuum and polish – the whole shebang? Thought so. Check your passport renewal date – maybe this needs updating, and you know how tedious those forms and the long waiting time can be. And if your passport doesn't need renewing – perhaps someone's close to you does. Does the anti-virus on your laptop need updating? Have you been clicking the 'ask me later' option when it asks you time and time again to update it? Well now's the time to sort it out! Maybe you need to clear up the memory on your laptop, tidy up the desktop or back up your documents, photos and music. Maybe you have an out-dated satellite navigation system for your car – update this online for the latest roundabouts and speed camera revisions – you'll appreciate it when you take your next trip and your old version tells you to drive through a ford or to do a U-turn on a mini-roundabout...! As you can see, we're getting quite a list already – and I'm sure you already had your own list brewing. Plus, don't forget, sorting out the mundane is a fantastic thing to accomplish during your Time Away from the Norm, as it will free up time for when you do return to work – am-a-zing!

Make a Song & a Dance about it!

I hate dancing. Don't have a dancing bone in my body. No rhythm. Nothing. And don't even get me started with my ability to sing. Those who have seen me have a go at the ol' karaoke from time to time will know what I'm talking about ;). "But everyone can sing and dance!" I hear you exclaim. No, really, not everyone can. But what I do agree with is that it certainly doesn't stop you from giving it a go! *Especially* when no-one's at home... who's going to know?! There's nothing quite like putting on an old disco classic and pratting around to a tune (hairbrush in hand), and giving it your all! Perhaps you have Sing Star Karaoke or a similar device – you can practise until the cows come home and be uber ready for that next cringe-worthy party when someone suggests that it's 'karaoooke time!' Because everyone knows it's not your singing ability that wins – it's *all* about hitting those notes at the right place and at the right time. Obviously, if you're highly intoxicated during your next karaoke shin-dig and you *still* manage to make a state of yourself, then I'm afraid I can't help you there ;).

But seriously, singing and dancing can really have a positive impact on your mood. There's no way that a Right Said Fred or Wham! tune can make you wear a frown on your face. I may be wrong, but in my experience I have found that an old-time favourite tune is an all-time winning tune and can do no wrong. It'll bring back some hilarious memories, remind you of people you may have forgotten about or lost touch with (and prompt you to get back in touch with them), and if at the very least it brings a momentary smile to your face, then I think it's damn well worth putting that record on. And don't forget all the health benefits too – singing increases lung capacity, boosts circulation and tones the abdom muscles – winner!

On a more tidying up / money making note, if you end up having a bit of a clear out and find that there are CDs you no longer want, then do not fret, as there are many websites including www.musicmagpie.co.uk that allow you to scan in the barcode of your CDs (and DVDs) and send them off in exchange for money (excuse me if you've already seen their many ads!). Or you could take the more traditional route of having a car-boot sale, donating them to your local charity store (Oxfam have specialist music stores), or simply giving them away to friends and family who you know will cherish that old Steps Greatest Hits CD of yours and put a smile on their face :).

Time for a Swap

Bored of the same unexciting views from your bedroom window? Tired of the local shops and its usual offerings? Fed up of your neighbours playing their music too loud again? Then a change in living environment may be the answer! A change in surroundings really does help put a new perspective on things and make a difference in how you feel. There are many websites out there offering a room and home swap and some of these even involve going abroad! If you've seen the film 'The Holiday' you'll know a bit about this and how much fun it can end up being. Naturally, Hollywood isn't reality and there are some practicalities about this approach, and you'll need to make sure that this is OK with those you're living with and whatnot. But if so, then hey, why not? You can do this for as long as you like – whatever works for you and the person you're doing the swap with.

If you're currently renting, and things haven't been working so great, then this could also be a great time to look for an alternative space to live, as there's nothing worse than living with people who cause you to feel unhappy or irritated – this can bring down your energy levels and leave you feeling down, which is not what Time Away from the Norm is intended for. Your living environment is of utmost importance and you may decide that now is the time to say farewell to those old housemates you've outgrown and to find some new people to bring some sparkle and Oomph back into your life. And with Time Away from the Norm being just that, you actually have the time to set up appointments and view different properties. You can really take your time, and often be the first to spot a new room on the market and get in there quickly! And if you do have to find a replacement for your own room; again, hey presto, you have the time to do this ;).

Your Culinary Side

Now cooking, I believe, is great fun when you have lots of time at hand. Really. Time and time again you get back from work late, and you throw something together which is quick and easy. Failing that, you may just re-heat something from the previous night (or the night before!), make something microwavable or dial up and order that trusty take-away. On the other hand, I may be completely wrong and you may in fact be a real whizz in the kitchen and have a highly nutritious, freshly cooked meal every night. If so – I salute you! But I know in reality this doesn't happen all the time. Well, now's your time to make amends :). And again, I'm not talking anything big or fancy – you don't have to put your Jamie or Delia hat on to succeed in the culinary department – you can just be yourself and have a bit of a dabble. Remember – it's not about precise measurements and buying the exact ingredients – it's more a case of guessing and improvising with what you have or see down at the market, and ultimately what you fancy at the time.

Whichever stage you're at, there's always room for improvement. So dust off your cookbook and try out a recipe, and if you don't have a recipe book, go online and Google a recipe you're interested in cooking. Perhaps ask a friend for a recommendation, go to your local library or pick out something suitable from a magazine or newspaper supplement; recipes are widely available. I'm also not talking cooking each day – 'Come Dine with Me' style – just whenever it takes your fancy, and perhaps just a dessert or a starter to begin with. Whatever it is, it'll serve you well for life and you may discover different techniques and tricks that you can apply from one dish to another, or perhaps discover a new cuisine entirely. And don't forget that you can make it as fun as you like – so pour yourself a glass of vino, slice up some cheese and indulge in the joy of cooking (and eating!). Who knows, next time it could be your friends begging to know the secret ingredient in that buonissimo lasagne dish of yours ;).

The Secret Garden

OK, I'll be the first to admit that gardening doesn't sound all too appealing – it's what seriously old people do when they retire, right? Wrong! Gardening truly is for *anyone*. And it's especially great if you're not one for going to the gym – gardening is really good exercise and your workout can be much closer to home than you realise, and you can also reap the benefits of learning new skills, lowering stress levels and lapping up ample vitamin D from being out in the sunlight. Fab! And don't forget, it's a really peaceful and tranquil activity to do too – great if you need a break from all the hecticity in your life.

You can be really creative and set up your garden in any way you like, including cultivating your very own organic garden, which can feed into your new found love for cooking! And with all that fresh air flowing in your lungs, digging and shovelling soil can have a really positive impact on how you feel, as well as helping to diminish any pent-up anger. It really is therapeutic – definitely give it a go! And if you don't have a garden – someone you know will have one and will absolutely want their lawn mown at the very least, so go give them a call!

Gardening was something I tried, quite possibly for the first time in my life, during my Time Away from the Norm, and I gained so much from it, but most notably patience. Not your most apparent benefit, I agree, but gardening really did teach me this. Gardening is not an activity which has instantaneous results, and there are various stages from planning and preparing the land, planting the seeds, all the way to monitoring and waiting for your creations to grow. It was well worth it though, and I felt a real sense of pride and accomplishment with what I'd produced. So take a deep breath and soak up the sounds, smells and colours of your garden, stand back and be inspired by fruitful creations. Bliss :).

DIY it

Ah, the good ol' joys of DIY. Again, an activity that absolutely anyone can do. And yes, absolutely anyone really does include *you* ;). DIY may involve re-wiring an old plug to other tasks that have needed doing for a few days to <ahem> a few years (yikes!). The sense of satisfaction you'll get from finally completing these tasks is fantastic. Not to mention how good you'll feel when you tell those around you what you've done! And the fact that you're improving your own living environment, whilst improving your DIY skills – well you can't go too wrong there ;).

And DIY really is a lot more than just building a bookshelf or makeshift wardrobe, and can stretch to painting various rooms around your home. How many times have you walked past your walls and thought 'wowsers, that could do with a bit of a lick of paint or two?' How many times have you planned to do some painting, but something just so happened to come up on that very same day...? I'm not even going to embarrass you by making you think how long it's been since you last gave the walls a once over. And if you're living in rented accommodation, perhaps check with your landlord first if it's OK with them – the likelihood is that they'll be happy that you're looking to improve the place. Some may even pay for the paint and brushes. Either way, painting is a fantastic way to utilise your energy (I always get the best night's sleep after painting!) and you can pump up the tunes and really get into it. Plus, it's something to be really proud of too – there's nothing quite like walking through your living room and thinking to yourself 'wow, *I* painted that.' Not to mention all the compliments you'll receive from visitors and those you live with. And remember it's not permanent – you can always change it back or repaint it if you don't like it, or paint it a new colour if you massively get into it ;).

And why not challenge yourself that step further? Why not make something with your bare hands? A strange concept, I know. It's surprising how little we physically make any more, but building or making something can be such a satisfying and rewarding project to have. And you really can make anything. You don't have to buy materials either, as you can often find scrap materials around your house, in people's skips (check with them first!), local shops – or perhaps someone you know has that odd palette of wood lying about. You can make a bedside table, a picture frame, a garden shed – you can literally be as ambitious as you like! Perhaps if you're new to all this, you could pick up something at your local DIY store to make or follow some instructions online until you pass the initial amateur stages. The key here is really giving it a go, because as you get used to the different materials – wood, steel, plastic and whatnot – you'll get different ideas for things you can make with them, and soon you'll have a handful of projects on the go and you won't know which one to pursue! Tip – make sure you don't leave a half made table or chair lying about...!

Arena's Top-Tip Chapter Summary

✓ Pull on the spring cleaning gloves, slap on some tunes and get your energy levels going with a good ol' fashioned clear-out and reshuffle

✓ It's dull, it's boring, but hey it's got to be done: sort out the admin in your life and free up some golden time for when you do go back to work

✓ Put your best foot forward and sing and dance away the blues to reap the benefits from your all-time fave tunes

✓ Do a Cameron Diaz and swap homes for a bit – it will help you see things from a whole new perspective, quite literally

✓ Maybe you're already a whizz in the kitchen and starting out is for amateurs – whatever stage you're at, have a go at sprucing up that culinary delight

✓ Take in some fresh air and get back to nature by having a dig around your back garden and getting stuck into some form of gardening

✓ Stretch your DIY skills by perhaps dabbling at something that bit more adventurous and daring, but don't forget to repair that dusty old clock whilst you're at it too

7. Get Out & About – Go Glocal!

Despite what you may already know about where you live, there's never been a better time to be out and about; meeting people, and getting to know your local and surrounding area that bit better. Whilst experiencing Time Away from the Norm it is easy to retract, become introverted and decide to stay indoors more. Going out may feel really quite daunting or challenging. Or perhaps it just seems a great deal easier to stay inside – you have everything you need there after all. The point is, quite frankly, that the less you venture out, the more difficult it becomes – like with anything in life, I guess. Anyway, I am here – armed with ideas to inspire you to make the small trips, to venture, to explore – because there's no replacement for a slice of the real world that we live in :).

Go Out & Rediscover!

Now there are many guide books out there telling you the A-Z of places to visit, so you really don't need me to tell you the specifics of being out and about and visiting places. But what I can do is *remind* you of the wonderful world that we live in! When was the last time you checked out a museum? Took a stroll around your local park? Checked out the local churches, gardens, side streets or galleries? The last time you got truly lost in a place, and were forced to use a map (*not* the one on your iPhone!) and to speak with people to navigate your way home? That feeling in the pit of your stomach at the realisation that you may be completely and utterly lost...? When was the last time you went to a tube, bus or tram stop that you've never been to before and gotten off and explored the spot? Eaten at a restaurant you wouldn't normally? Explored an old pub off the beaten track? Stopped at a café you've passed a thousand times but went to the nearest chain instead just to be sure you got your Chai Tea Latte with cinnamon on top...? I may be harping on a bit, I appreciate, but my point is that there really are a lot of things that we end up missing and dismissing – places we never see in our own towns and cities, and then there are the places that we always see but don't properly utilise and experience. Remember when you bump into a tourist and they've been in the UK for only a handful of days, yet they've managed to see more in those few days than you've seen in your entire life? The way you can feel the heat rising up your face as they ask you what you think of Trinity College in Cambridge or you struggle to remember the birthplace of Shakespeare and that famous ol' stadium in London with the big, curved arch... now's *really* the time to be getting out there and rediscovering!

A lot of towns (more than you realise!) will have a tourist information centre. As your first stop, this could be a great place to check out as part of the initial 'getting started' phase. They can give you maps and a bit of history behind that statue you glaringly ignored each day as you walked on by. I used to walk past a lion statue in Reading all the time and had no idea that it represented the deaths of 329 men in the Berkshire regiment and that the lion was named after a village in Afghanistan (Maiwand). It's always really interesting to find out things like that. Maybe check out other local towns in your area, walking paths, cycle routes or perhaps just find out about the history of the town you reside in – you'll pick up an interesting fact or two, that's for sure. Happy exploring!

Confessions of a Shopaholic

Now shopping really doesn't float my boat, but daytime shopping, I must admit, is actually pretty bearable, and dare I say it... <gulp> fun! The shops are reasonably empty and you can actually ask the assistants to help you. You don't have to queue for the changing rooms, and new stock often comes in during the week so you're more likely to get the style and the size you're after. It's just generally a lot less stressful and hence that bit more enjoyable. And I know some people simply *love* nothing better than a good shopping trip and will revel in the idea of some extra time for retail therapy. So if this is you – get those bags at the ready and bring out the shopaholic in you! Plus it's a great workout too – think of the number of calories you'll be burning and how strong your calf and upper arm muscles will become? Goodbye bingo wings, hello super-toned arms! So whether it's Gateshead, Meadowhall, Brent Cross or the Bullring – get your walking boots on and put your best (shopping!) foot forward!

You can get yourself a completely new style, try on clothes you wouldn't normally go for and discover a brand new look – winner! Not very impressed with your high street offering? Don't forget all those clothes markets, boutiques, charity and independent stores – there are plenty of these around and they offer you that original design and cut to set you aside from the crowd. And if you're still not impressed (you're a tough cookie!), then why not look to make or customise your own clothes and accessories? Now this is dead easy, and can be done quite simply – adding in a few rips and tears, an extra bow or by tie dying those jeans. If the weather's a bit warm – turn your shoddy jeans into shorts. Frayed edges are all the rage :). Perhaps you're a bit lazy, or maybe just unsure of what would look right on you, then a personal shopper may be the answer. Most major department stores will offer this service, and if they don't – most assistants will be happy to offer their advice and professional opinion – it's their job after all! This is great if you want a new look or just to try something a bit different. Plus the service is free, so definitely take advantage of it!

If you're a bit like me, and clothes shopping isn't really your idea of fun and games, it's good to remember the other types of shops out there that still come under the umbrella of 'shopping', but may be of more interest to you: electrical, sports, photography, homeware, stationary, garden centres and camping stores – it's not *all* about clothes shopping.

Perhaps you have birthday presents to buy, a Secret Santa present to source, your aunt's getting married, your sister's had a baby, your cat's turned eight. Whatever the occasion, you've got shopping to do. Maybe you really want to make the most of your Time Away from the Norm, as you know that it's for a limited time only (roll up, roll up!), and you want to buy gifts that you know you'll have to buy in the upcoming months. This is a great thing to do with your Time Away from the Norm, as you can actually take the time to think of really fitting presents – you can buy something really meaningful (or just plain hilarious!). Whatever it is, it's bound to get noticed and will shine above all those other mundane gifts that are often bought at the last minute or at a petrol station on Christmas Eve. Not by you though, *of course* :). Obviously I'm making a few assumptions here, and your gifts may already be astounding. If so – get you! But for those of you who handed out those Woolworth's vouchers that now can't be spent (doh!), now's the time to make a few amends ;).

It needn't be expensive either, as you'll have the time to shop around between stores, not merely picking up the first item you see just because you 'need a grey jumper.' You can combine shopping at your local mall with online shopping, particularly with those items where substitutes aren't readily available and you can indeed get the best price. Power to the consumer! And don't forget retail outlets too for that bargain-bustin' buy. Also, if you're making a big purchase, like a laptop perhaps, you can really take your time to speak with sales assistants, do your own research, chat to your techie mates, try a few different laptops and maybe have one made bespoke to meet all your needs. Whatever it is you're buying, now's the time to really be able to take a step back, have a good think and buy the best that's on offer for you.

If nothing else, you'll also be surprised at the number of people out shopping in the middle of the day – lots of other people who aren't merely doing the '9 to 5', or like you may be experiencing

Time Away from the Norm. Remember, there are a lot of us out there. An army of us out there – you most certainly are not alone :).

Bog Off!

OK, not literally, but I mean in terms of packing your bags and going away for a few days on the spur of the moment. Maybe with others you know, or perhaps by yourself. You may have friends and family based in other countries, and depending on your time and budget, you could pay them a visit. It's worth informing your workplace and those around you that you'll be going away in case they need to contact you, but otherwise with so many airlines and websites offering last minute budget deals, pick a country at random and off you go – the world really is your oyster!

If you don't know anyone abroad, and no-one around you has any annual leave left to take, then fear not! Going away by yourself really is the answer. You may have tried this before, and have really reaped the benefits of this – some 'me' time is some of the most valuable time you can spend, and this alone is reason enough to do it. If it's not, then again, worry not, for I am armed with reasons ahoy! Travelling by yourself makes you more at ease with yourself; to really be able to enjoy your own company and to be happy and comfortable with who you are. It increases your self-perception and undoubtedly your confidence, simply because you're 'out there' – you are forced to speak with people, whether it's regarding getting a cab or speaking with hotel, bar and train station staff. It forces you to socialise and meet with people, and you'll be truly amazed at how many people do travel independently. Plus you're your own boss – you can do what you want, when you want, whenever you want... bliss! Don't know where to go? Grab a globe, give it a spin, and see where it stops! And no, you don't have to be in a Hollywood movie to commit such an act – the world really is at arm's reach ;).

If the thought of going away by yourself still sends shudders through you, then that's completely fine – it doesn't have to be for everyone. It's good to stretch yourself into uncomfortable situations at times, but if it's going to send you into frantic mode, then you can reduce the stress by perhaps going through an organisation where your itinerary is organised up front, and you can even pick the age group you'd like to go away with, if you like. A volunteering trip is another way to ensure that you'll have someone at the other end, and these getaways can provide an invaluable way to make a difference to a local community and bring endless benefits to other people and yourself through the process. I did something similar in Nepal for three months and had an incredible time. I was fortunate enough to witness some of the finest, breath-taking scenery each day, meet and help some amazing, unforgettable people and experience a fascinating new culture and language all at the same time. I really couldn't dig and recommend doing something like this anymore if I tried. Really.

Yes, I'm harping on about volunteering, but it can be a cheap way to get away – you can find an organisation that hosts and feeds you in exchange for free work (what a great exchange!). And one that springs to mind is Wwoof (www.wwoof.org) who are a charity teaching people about organic growing and low-impact lifestyles through hands-on experience – and again they are based on a global level. If money's an issue then you could look to get some free accommodation by couch-surfing (www.couchsurfing.org) where you can stay on a different couch each night (or a number of nights) and meet some fab and interesting people whilst doing so. They represent virtually every country, and it works by creating your own profile and searching through a database depending upon your criteria. And then there's the European Voluntary Service, which is open to eighteen to thirty year olds within the EU who would like to do a fully funded volunteer placement in Europe for up to a year. Give them a Google ;).

Perhaps you're looking for a few days to get away from it all; to re-charge in a natural environment with no phones going off, no cars, just the natural sounds of the birds tweeting and the breeze in the air. Well if so, an eco-centre may be the answer! There are many of these around the world, and one that I went to visit was La Casita Verde (www.casitaverde.com) in Ibiza, which is a model ecology education centre that is operated by volunteers and open for visitors on Sundays. "An ecology-centre in Ibiza?" I hear you exclaim. "Ibiza – the land of chunder, booze and all things chavalicious?" I hear you question. And rightly so – despite the image it may have, Ibiza island is simply astounding and the eco-centre is set in a stunning location in a beautiful valley and can really help you unwind and ease up any tension, whilst meeting some truly fantastic people and learning all about how a more sustainable way of living is within reach of every one of us.

Whatever you end up doing, and however you end up doing it – the point is that a change in environment can really have a positive impact on how you feel about things. I remember my time in Nepal really taught me to take things one step at a time and completely forced me to live in the moment, as everything was so different – it simply demanded my full attention and energy. It took me away from my current situation and gave me a whole new perspective – a better one. If anything, going away will help you see that there's a big wide world out there, and although you and your issues may be central to what's going on in your life right now, it'll help you to realise and see the bigger picture – and to ultimately not miss out on the world!

Organise a Trip Away

Aside from doing a slightly different type of travel trip, nothing quite beats a good ol' fashioned holiday. This section examines this further and looks at the upcoming months and utilising your Time Away from the Norm to get that trip booked in! This can be a trip planned for when you return to work, or perhaps if you're not working you may want that getaway in your calendar to act as a motivator for you – to help you with your job hunting, for instance. And if your friends never get round to sorting out a break away, then you can be the one to take charge and make it happen! Or better still, if you're not Mr or Mrs Organised, or just don't fancy organising it – get your group of friends together, identify the tasks at hand – so flights, accommodation, dates, activities, sight-seeing and whatnot – and delegate them out. This way, everyone is responsible for an important element in making the holiday happen and therefore has to complete their allocated task/s. Because you can't have accommodation and no means of transport to get to your holiday, let's face it!

And if you really don't fancy an actual holiday as such, then do something small. Maybe have a weekend break away at the beach – UK beaches are really something pretty special, but are often forgotten about as Kos and Alicante beckon. Maybe you could go camping down by your local forest or up in the Lake District? Why not take a road trip? And no, it's not something that only American high school kids do – you too can do this! Get a couple of mates, your cousin, your neighbour – whoever, and take a trip round the country. How many people neglect the beauty of the UK or have not yet fully explored it? Can you safely say that you've experienced all the charms of Warwick, Edinburgh, Cornwall, Windsor, the New Forest, Stonehenge or even good old London town? I know I can't. And those are just a few examples. Maybe you could go to all the towns where you have friends and family you haven't seen in an age and pay them a visit? Imagine how pleased they'll be to see you? And anyway, who needs Route 66 when you have the M6! Rock on ;).

So you already have a trip booked? Excellent. Well now's the time to do some research, which is a great way to get really excited about your hol, not to mention the time it will save when you're out there and you already know your Colosseum from your Piazza Navona. And if you're really smart, you would have sought out exactly where the key sights are, the opening times, best times to visit and booked your tickets online with a substantial discount! Clever clogs ;). Prior research is also great for getting recommendations from those you know and from online forums – the best places to eat, where to catch a show, how to get on a free walking tour or hear about a really picturesque square that you may have otherwise missed out on. Maybe have some lessons if you're going on a skiing or other type of sporting holiday, and get in a bit of practise early on. You can get some guide books out from your local library, read online guides, and if there's something in particular you're interested in – for instance info on the gay scene, things to do with kids or religious monuments and archaeological sites, then it's worth getting the low-down early on. Insider knowledge is definitely the way forward!

Take a Sabbatical

If you find going away really does help you de-stress and take your focus away from your troubles and woes, then perhaps it's worth looking into this on a longer term perspective. Now I know this may not work for everyone at such short notice; your circumstances may not allow it or your workplace may not be flexible on this front, for instance. But it is something seriously worth considering, as taking some time away in a different environment could be exactly what your body needs, and it may be a conversation worth having out loud, (not just inside your head). We all know how happy, relaxed and content we feel after a good break away. Well, why not do just this, but for a longer period of time? Perhaps you've always wanted to motorcycle round South America ('Motorcycle Diaries' style!), reach the summit of Mount Kilimanjaro or take the Trans-Siberian train, but never really had the time or opportunity to do such a thing. Maybe your Time Away from the Norm is the perfect and opportune time for this? A sabbatical could be absolutely anything – I know a couple who decided to pack their lives into a 4wd and drive from Banbury down to South Africa and back, sleeping in a tent on top of their jeep. They had an amazing time! And remember, you don't have to do anything substantial like that. Simply being away in a completely different environment can be a healer in itself. You can just head somewhere you've been before that you really enjoyed and felt totally relaxed at, and travel around there for a while. Imagine what wonders a few months away could do for you?

Note, that a sabbatical or any kind of going away should not be seen as 'running away' from your issues and problems. If you've got skeletons and concerns, then sadly they'll still be waiting for you when you get back. And, as easy as it may be not to think about them when you're out scuba diving and camel racing, they'll be waiting for you when you have those small pockets of quiet time; on a coach journey perhaps or when you go to sleep at night. Those lingering, haggling thoughts that go round and round in your head aren't that easy to get rid of, I know. And it's worth sitting down and perhaps speaking with people about whether a sabbatical could be of real benefit to you or not. But depending on your own circumstances, maybe you could attempt to sort some things out before going away? This could be a great motivator in getting sorted. Or maybe put a plan in place that you agree to action when you get back? So almost like making a deal and a promise with yourself. Or perhaps going away really could be the answer. Only you have the answer. Not just a tube of Smarties ;).

Arena's Top-Tip Chapter Summary

✓ Get out and rediscover your town and local surroundings – you'll soon pick up an interesting route, fact and more!

✓ It doesn't matter how much you despise it – there's always some type of shopping to be done, so head out now to avoid those oozing weekend crowds

✓ In the words of Madonna – grab your bags and go on a holiday – sign up to a programme, do it solo, volunteer abroad – get out of town for that fresh holiday feeling

✓ Use your time away to properly plan and organise a holiday, and ensure that it actually takes place!

✓ Taking a longer period of time off work in the form of a sabbatical may be something worth exploring if you're someone that really reaps the benefits of being away

8. Breaking Loose From The Norm!

Time Away from the Norm involves a bit of breaking loose from the Norm too ;). OK, it's about doing the sensible, doing the sorting; those things on your to-do list that need to be done. But it's not all about that. No, it's about doing those things that you wouldn't normally do and perceiving your time off as a kind of 'borrowed' time – having the mind-set of thinking 'I may never have this time off again!' Once you have this mentality – there really are no limits to what you can be doing – and remember; keep it fresh ;).

The Random & the Obscure (because it's Fun)

Think the obscure... and do the obscure! Think of the most random of activities that you've always fancied doing – the weird, the haphazard, the cheeky – something you've heard of or seen someone do and thought 'oooh, that's a bit different... wouldn't mind giving that a go', and then quickly dismissing the thought as speedily as it appeared. Ever had that? Well now's your chance to go back to it and actually give it a go! Experiencing Time Away from the Norm really is about doing something different. After all – it is borrowed time – you would normally be at work; you'd be doing what you normally do in your normal day-to-day normal life, normally... But things are different now – and utilising your time to do something you've always 'kinda fancied, but never quite got round to' – well it would just be plain wrong to turn around and walk away from an opportunity like that! Right?

And if you need a bit of inspiration, then fear not, as ideas (as always!) are at hand! Why not try your hand at a bit of poi, korfballing, juggling, origami, pole dancing, skydiving, aerobatic flying, kite-surfing, sphereing, quad biking, calligraphy, canyoning, bungee jumping, rappelling, ham radioing, dog training, figure skating, zip wiring, bouldering, coasteering... phew! And if you don't know what some of them are – look them up ;). And if you're not sure which one to do, why not write up a realistic selection of ones that you could feasibly do, fold them up, whack them into a hat and pick one out... and tada – that's your answer! And if it's a challenge to you, then all the better! As without setting challenges, it's difficult to get excited about the world, and these challenges ultimately push us forward and get us out there in the world. Do it!

Brand New you

'Out with the old and in with the new.' You know how it is. Horrendously clichéd as it may sound, recreating and giving yourself a new style or image can work wonders for you, *especially* when experiencing Time Away from the Norm. In a way, a new you can symbolise the different stages you are going through, metaphorically and literally. So, maybe you've always fancied that different cut or look to your locks and tresses? Or wouldn't it be great to have something quite radical and different? Celebrities are usually a great starting point for something like this – Google 'celebrity hairstyles' for instant inspiration. And remember you don't have to copy them completely – so if it's Matt Damon's fringe or Pink's wild streak of colour you envy (random!), then mention it to your hairdresser. Maybe even discuss with them what would suit you best – sometimes the shape of your face, the 'behaviour' of your hair and how much time you wish to spend on your barnet each day can dictate what you end up with. I remember having around seven inches of my hair cut into the tiniest of bobs and could not have felt better as a result. It took a while and it didn't really help that my hairdresser kept saying "are you *sure* you want to take so much off...?" and "you're *soo* brave doing this" – but it all made for a fun afternoon! Plus, I didn't have my glasses on, so couldn't really see what was going on anyway... ;)!

OK, so maybe cutting your hair isn't exactly what you're after. Maybe you love your hair just the length it is. Perhaps dying it could make all the difference. Obviously, you need to be careful with what you do for a living – dying your hair purple or green may look ace, but may not be appropriate if you're working in a customer facing environment, for example. But sometimes having a bit of a change is just plain fun. It just keeps things that bit interesting, I guess. Maybe you've always fancied getting a part of your body pierced or tattooed. Live life on the edge (or '*by* the edge' as someone I know always tells me!). You can spend time designing your tattoo and make it as simple or as complicated as you like. Big or small. And if you've had a tattoo before, you'll appreciate the time it takes to choose the design to get it *juuust* right.

If you're just not into changing your physical appearance, then that really is quite alright :). But perhaps look to change routines you already have. OK, so you brush your teeth twice a day, so what? You can make changes to this routine – replace a regular brush with an electric one, start to floss your teeth, use a mouthwash – maybe you do this already, but could perhaps look to change your dental products to suit your needs better? And that's just one aspect of your daily routine to examine. I know these are things I hadn't really bothered with before, but they really are important – you do them every day (I hope!), after all, so fully worth the investment of time and thought.

Blag! Abuse! The Beauty of the Daytime Matinee...

'Nothing in life comes for free' they tell you! Know the phrase? You use and hear it all the time. Well shun that! Because everyone has a friend who works somewhere who has an ex who knows someone whose tortoise knows the perfect person who can get you something for free! Some of these treats may only be available in the daytime, or may just be those type of freebies that you didn't take advantage of whilst you were working full-time. It could be anything from free entry to a museum to a free trial of a new product. Recent free examples I remember are having a tour of Wembley Stadium through a housemate, and watching Enron at the theatre as a friend had cleverly signed up to www.showfilmfirst.com, but couldn't make the show as it was in the middle of the day and it was too late for her to take time off work. Winner!

It really is out there! There are various free things available, but often time is the essence and we just don't have enough of it. So if you fancy getting a free or cut-price haircut (normally by a trainee) at a high-end stylist, then do it! Perhaps you want to test out that nice flash car you've seen at the local garage. Well now's your chance! And getting a stunning new mullet or doing a flash car trial are just two of the areas that you can take advantage of in terms of freebies. People are training in all different fields all the time, and will be looking for potential free clients to practise on. If you know what service you're after, you can Google this and source out your freebie. If, on the other hand you're looking for inspiration, then just keep your eyes peeled! Noticeboards, newspapers, lampposts, speaking with people at your local shop – these are some of the best ways to find out about such opportunities.

And although not everything in life is free, do not forget the daytime matinee – this is a cheaper alternative to the often sky-high prices that are charged the rest of the time for many services. The cinema is the obvious place that comes to mind, but there are lots – the theatre, bowling, ice-skating, indoor skiing, as well as train and travel tickets being cheaper off-peak. So do take advantage of these when you can. And again *remind* people about this – remind those around you how empty the beach is in the middle of the week, and how cheap an off-peak train ticket is – they'll soon be looking to get rid of those extra days of annual leave faster than you can say Harry Ramsden!

Market research is another great way to a grab a swift freebie. There are many companies out there looking to try and test their products, services, promotions and advertising on you – the consumer, to find out your views and motivations. This can be in the form of a questionnaire (paper or online) or through an in-depth interview or focus group. The latter face-to-face options often involve a cash incentive for the 'inconvenience' and tend to feed you well too – bargainaceous! You sit in a room with around six-ten individuals and are guided through questions and activities on the product / service / concept at hand. As well as the obvious financial incentive, you get to meet other people in your area who may also be experiencing Time Away from the Norm, who you could potentially look to meet with again. Which is great, because there's nothing like meeting someone who's in a similar boat to yourself. There's also the buzz of learning about potential future products and ideas, and it may get your own creative side beating too. So it really is worth finding out about market research in your local area! I know that some towns and areas have specialist agencies recruiting people to participate in research (a quick Internet search should produce these) – so *even* easier for you! Obviously, if you already work in market research, then this is a no-go area, but hey you already knew that ;).

Re-re-wind

Childhood is often the happiest time in a person's life. Now, I know this isn't true for everyone, and childhood is normally a mixed kettle of fish for all, but there are some elements of childhood that will always stand out as being pretty good – at least in the sense that real responsibilities didn't properly exist, and time didn't fly by as ridiculously fast as it can often do now. Becoming a kid again doesn't mean behaving like a child again – far from. It just means enjoying the things that as a child you perhaps did, and this can be easily recreated in many forms. Simply producing a makeshift obstacle course with your sofas and cushions to reconstruct the game show 'Fun House' (remember Pat Sharpe?!) can be enough to do the trick. *So* much fun! Maybe by watching some kids'

TV – you'll be surprised at how funny and light-hearted some of the shows can be and how they can really lift your mood – 'Drake and Josh', 'iCarly' and 'The Suite Life of Zack and Cody' are a few of my personal favourites ;).

Collecting shells along the beach has been shown to be highly therapeutic and it's something you may remember doing as a kid. Perhaps a day at the beach could help recreate this moment – simply walk along, pay attention to the shells, select the ones that take your fancy and really focus and concentrate solely on doing just this. As a kid you could probably do this without thinking about much else, and be completely absorbed in the task at hand. Right now it may seem that bit harder than normal, but try it anyway. And if getting to the beach for the day really isn't feasible, why not recreate your own in your back garden? A sandpit and small paddling pool to dip your toes in is all you need or maybe just get the hose pipe out. Alternatively, head down to the local park. Other child-like activities can include playing board games, building Lego or playing with plasticine and Play-Doh. You may have your own memories and ideas of what you did in your childhood that you'd like to have a go at doing again. Making chocolate Cornflake cakes is another one of my favourites. Yum! Whatever you do, the idea is to help you feel carefree and relaxed again by taking you back to another point in your life. Don't lose the spirit of the child!

Get Down with the Beat

Now we've looked at how music can be a great way to lift your mood at home by having a bit of a bop and a sing-along, as well as helping you to earn the odd extra bob by selling your unwanted CDs. But here we will explore the musical sounds of the underground in more detail...

So, if you're already a music fan, you'll know how significant a great tune can be in your life – how it can get you humming and toe-tapping, all the way to full blown jumping and jamming. You may also be familiar with how an old, fab tune can remind you of happy times; bring back some great memories and really put that smile back on your face. For those reasons, and those reasons alone, it's worth listening to some of your all-time fave CDs to lift your mood and give you that energy booster. And no, listening to slow, sad music, regardless of how big a Mariah fan you are is a real no-no. And yes, as amazing as The Smiths are, songs like 'Girlfriend in a Coma' and 'Heaven knows I'm Miserable Now' will probably not lift your mood – and you and I both know that. So stick with the happy beats – you'll soon notice the difference it can have on you :).

Perhaps to have a bit of a change, it's worth having a browse through your friends' CD or online collections and giving a couple of those albums a whirl. You'll be surprised at how a change in music can help you discover new artists and bands, and really expand your taste and knowledge deep down in your core, musical buds. And don't just stop with your friends – ask other people you know, including your parents, if they're still around. Your parents are actually a great source for music, and you'll often find the original versions of songs that you're currently listening to – or they may have that bootleg version of 'Yellow Submarine' or an original Bob Marley album on vinyl. Now that's pretty cool :).

As well as widening your music taste through other people's musical collections, don't forget the radio. And as fantastic as Scott Mills is in the afternoon of Radio 1, it's good to broaden who you would normally listen to by changing stations every now and again. As, let's be fair, it doesn't matter which radio station you listen to, the songs are pretty much on repeat throughout the day and week – not great when you're looking to broaden your musical horizon. www.england.fm is an amazing website for alternative radio stations – it has everything from Radio Caroline to Solar Radio – definitely have a browse and a listen. Plus this site is great if you have varied taste in music – so if you fancy a bit of rock to get you going in the morning, that bit of jazz in the afternoon and some mellow chill-out R&B in the evening, then you can pick your radio station accordingly. Great stuff.

So you've discovered tunes that you wouldn't normally listen to and you're switching radio stations quicker than you can say Terry Wogan. So what's next? Well, when was the last time you updated your MP3, iPod or other music player that you use on the go? Either way, there comes a point when you need to change and replenish, and with all these new tunes on the agenda, there's never been a better time than now! So get uploading and go out for a speed walk with your new bling tunes playing – there's no greater feeling than listening to some tunes when you're out and about to put that extra boost in your step and wiggle in your hips ;).

Another fun thing I really enjoy doing, and did a lot of during my Time Away from the Norm, is making CD compilations. This can make a fab gift for someone or you may simply like to put a collection of songs together to share with others more generally. Whilst sifting through your music collection you may come across some tunes and artists you haven't listened to in a while, and fancy putting some songs together simply for yourself! Perhaps a wake-up CD to get you going in the morning, some tunes to do some tidying-up or exercise to, or perhaps some chill-out tunes to relax to and just generally have on in the background. You may like to put a collection of songs together that remind you of a particular occasion or time in your life – of a holiday, drunken school nights out, a stag do, or a journey you've undertaken. I made a CD of some music festival tunes, as this is one of the times when I feel I'm at my happiest. Whatever it is, capture it on CD, so whatever mood you're in, you'll musically have the ammunition to put yourself in a better mood. Maybe record a CD with your own voice? If you don't have your own songs then sing someone else's and record it. Go on, have a bit of fun with it ;). For inspiration, Chris Moyles has his own parody CDs and they're *hilarious* – give them a spin!

Get your Creative Juices Flowing!

I understand this isn't for everyone, but something that can prove to be very useful during your Time Away from the Norm is getting your creative being beating. Endless studies have proven that the right side of the brain; the creative side, is often not utilised as much as it should be, particularly as we venture into adulthood. And as with exercise and other types of tasks you need to concentrate on, being creative can really take the focus away from what else is going on in your life, and help use this energy in a positive way to create something visual and tangible. And being creative doesn't mean painting Van Gogh style, it simply means playing around and having a go – grabbing a paint brush, an oil pastel, a pencil or a felt tip pen is really all you need. This is also useful as a form of art therapy to yourself – expressing how you feel imaginatively and spontaneously, and really letting your subconscious feelings and emotions out. It has also been shown to have inherent healing powers and can improve mental wellbeing. Worth a shot, surely?

If this sounds all a bit too arty farty for you, or you are still adamant that you do not have a creative bone within you, then there are other types of creative exercises you can try. Perhaps buy some clay at your local arts and crafts store and have a play around with it. It's amazing what you can end up making – and we're not just talking about your average coil mug that you may remember from your school days. Instead you can produce a sculpture, a vase, a plaque or just something very abstract. Clay also has a uniquely therapeutic quality to it, which can help settle and calm, and it can help retain your attention for hours. I always find it to be such an interesting, ever-changing texture. And you never know, this could be a great way to start doing some ceramics, and you could soon be re-creating the scenes from 'Ghost' in no time ;) Demi Moore, eat your heart out!

The opportunities really are endless – maybe you just want to grab a few magazines and make a bit of a collage. A photo collage is also an idea, which could double up as a great gift for somebody. Perhaps it's the Christmas season and you can set yourself a card-making project – how surprised and pleased will people be to receive a home-made card from you, as opposed to your average high street number? Whatever you end up doing, my point is that it doesn't have to be anything fancy or substantial – it's just about seeing what you have around you, utilising these materials and really giving arts and crafts a go. Go have a stab at it!

Digital Watch

So you have all those seasons of DVDs that you've always wanted to watch – well now is your time to seize the opportunity and have a bit of a DVD-marathon! How many times have you been recommended different shows, normally American ones, which have at least 28 series and you're like 'when will I honestly have the time to watch all of these?!' Tada :)! So pop the kettle on, grab some biccies and hit the play button. Bliss. I remember having adrenaline pumping for hours after watching the incredible Jack Bauer perform a stunt too many in

'24' during my Time Away from the Norm! Exciting times :). And for those of you who are proper TV series fanatics and have watched simply everything out there (wowsers!), then if you don't already do so, it may be worth signing up for film rentals, which often offer a free month's trial (or more if you're lucky!). These are normally run online, and you can borrow films and games, and have them delivered to your door. No late fees and charges, and they really can help you switch off to another galaxy far, far away...

As well as all those films and TV series you've been looking to catch-up on, don't forget the ones that are already out there. 4OD and the BBC iPlayer are both fantastic ways to discover and catch-up on one-off shows, dramas and documentaries that you may not have previously considered, or had the time for. And if you're feeling a bit down, then funny films, sitcoms and cartoons can be a great way to help beat the blues. They instantly make you laugh, lift your mood and generally help you feel good. 'Little Miss Sunshine', 'Happy Gilmore' and 'Life of Brian' are some that instantly come to mind, which will help get you started. But I'm sure you have some of your own 'ol' time faves' too ;). Perhaps also ask friends and family for inspiration – everyone has a cracker of a film that they'd love to recommend! Another idea is to consider different sports channels (you might discover a new sport you like!), the debate channels (these are great at getting the mind thinking!), as well as the film channels... so get those fingers exercising on your remote! Now although I'm not advocating watching obscene amounts of TV in isolation (really!) and ignoring all my other tips – just remember that it's all about mixing it up and having a variety of things on the go. You know what I mean ;).

Lingo it Up!

Add some new words to your vocabulary to brighten it up! Tired of saying the same thing in exactly the same way at exactly the same time? Do you use the same phrases, expressions and exclamations, time and time again...? Well, having Time Away from the Norm enables you to change all of that! Perhaps you need some invigorating new words to throw into a convo – a few adjectives to really illustrate your point – some words that more accurately express what you are trying to convey instead of a more general word you would normally tend to use. Maybe you could be creative and come up with your own words – perhaps shorten words or take the first half of one word you quite like and take the end of another one you fancy and merge them together. And no it's not speaking like a teenager – far from. What it's really about is using language in a clever and interesting manner, and taking the effort to truly convey what you're trying to say. Not to mention brightening up your speech from the same old mundane words to say something quite interesting and articulate. As frankly, using the same words time and time again can get quite, <yawn>, a bit bor-ing really. A thesaurus is a great way to get started as is a dictionary when you come across words you've read or heard that you don't understand or aren't quite sure of. It's all about making that bit more of a conscious effort with your speech. And if nothing else, you'll be a sure winner in that next game of Scrabble you end up playing ;).

Get a Pet

Watched the film 'Beethoven' and always fancied getting a dog? 'Finding Nemo' hit a nerve and you wanted to get some tropical fish? Or perhaps 'Ratatouille' inspired you to get some mice (*not* the ones that already live in your house...!). Whatever the animal, whatever the inspiration – getting a pet can have many great benefits to you, some of which may not be immediately apparent. Simply stroking a pet can have a very therapeutic effect on you how you feel, immediately helping you feel more calm and relaxed. A pet gives you a sense of duty and responsibility – you need to feed, clean and take care of it. Naturally, check that those you live with are happy to have an extra member to the household – no point getting a cat if your housemate's allergic to the hair, for example ;).

If you live in a place with no garden, a dog may be out the question, but don't let this stop you from getting a pet, as gerbils, hamsters and fish are all lower-maintenance animals that you can keep and look after even when your Time Away from the Norm comes to an end. And this is obviously a really key point to bear in mind, as one day your Time Away from the Norm will inevitably end, or at the very least differ. Circumstances change. Whatever happens, your pet will still be with you, so you need to see this as a long-term commitment. If it really isn't feasible for you to get an animal, then perhaps look to take care of your friend's pet for a few days. Or visit a local farm in your area. You'll be surprised at how many farms there actually are. I found two in my area quite easily – it was just something I'd never thought to look for before. Maybe even have a day out at the zoo! Being around animals can really bring about positive effects in your mood and influence how you feel, so it's worth looking into and pursuing. I find having an animal to talk to around the house to be really helpful. They never answer back at you(!), and sometimes speaking to someone without having any interruptions can honestly be a great way to figure things out. Brilliant.

Volunteering as a dog walker is also an excellent way to reap the benefits of having a dog, but without the full-time commitment of owning one. And it's a fantastic way to get into a routine and get the fresh air pumping into your lungs – you can explore new routes and areas you didn't know existed and meet new people at the same time. There are different ways in which you can become a dog walker: through a neighbour, a local animal rescue centre (they are likely to let you help out in other ways too) or perhaps just by advertising yourself as a free dog walker in your local library, corner shop etc. There are also charities that set up dog walking including the Cinnamon Trust who pair you up with someone in your local area, normally with someone who is housebound or terminally ill and need help with looking after their pet/s. You can apply to do this online (www.cinnamon.org.uk), and you'll be helping to make a real difference to the lives of the vulnerable simply by walking their dog. Now that's a good deed if ever I heard one!

Go back to your Roots

Try going on a voyage of rediscovery and tracing back your ancestors! This can be quite a daunting or exhilarating task – whatever your take. But is really worth the effort – who knows what you will discover? You could do a family tree and start with the obvious, and then make a few phone calls to relatives to fill in the gaps. It could really help you reconnect again. To start, maybe get a big sheet of paper and start drawing out the connections you already know – you may think you have a small family, but actually have quite a large one. You may also need to go to the library to find out further information about your family if you don't personally have access to such info, so do bear this in mind.

And whilst you're at it, why not meet with old members of your family – older people love re-telling stories of 'days gone by', so if they're still about then do get them involved – it can actually be really interesting, and you'll learn so much about history generally and how things have changed. It's such a discovery to make, and some of the stories that come about can be absolutely hilarious or just plain simple eye-openers. And won't it be great to have those memories and stories to then pass down to future generations? Beautiful.

Arena's Top-Tip Chapter Summary

✓ Really think outside the box and pick a random and obscure activity that takes your fancy... take a deep breath and take the plunge!

✓ Whether it's a change in hairstyle, a new routine or otherwise – keep things interesting by re-inventing yourself

✓ Take advantage of free and reduced novelties available during the day, and through friends and family who can bag and arrange that nifty freebie for you

✓ Take a trip down memory lane, and remember and recreate some of the good times from your childhood days

✓ As well as listening to your own (happy) beats, explore some new tunes through different avenues and see what you discover

✓ Reawaken your creative soul by opening yourself up to the expressive world of arts and crafts

✓ Have a DVD marathon and play catch-up by whipping through those various seasons of box sets you'd previously missed out on

✓ Give your speech a makeover by sprinkling some new words into your vocab to dazzle those you converse with

✓ Having a pet to look after gives you a great sense of focus and commitment outside of yourself and provides great (fluffy!) company

✓ Use your time to examine your family history and fill in the blanks on all those ancient ancestors of yours

9. "Hi Ho, Hi Ho, It's Off To Work We Go!"

Work fills around a third of our daily lives. And when you're facing Time Away from the Norm, it's very normal to feel a strong sense of void. In some cases you are filled with an extra 60 hours a week to contend with, which is quite a substantial amount of time. So it may be worth looking at some work related alternatives that you can do in your spare time to help create some structure to your own working week Norm. The next few pages provide a few pointers in how you can achieve this.

Volunteering

Now this equals a highly underrated area. We often forget that we have such great value in the world: that our actions and contributions really do count, and by volunteering we're amplifying our positive notions to those around us and our environment. And it doesn't matter how low and worthless you may feel during your Time Away from the Norm – the world really does need *you!* Your positive input adds real value and contributes to our planet, and volunteering can often act as a strong reminder of *how* less fortunate other people can be.

To get started, most towns will have a volunteering centre – often on your local high street. It's worth popping in and looking at any suitable vacancies, or if they have one – checking on their website for the latest vacancies, if that's easier. You are normally told to fill in a form indicating your preferences as to the type of work you'd be interested in doing – be it working with children, the elderly, the environment, construction, the local circus, painting... the opportunities are highly varied and can be quite random at times! You can do the odd day, a one-off event, or something on a part-time basis each week. Perhaps if you're a real eager beaver you could look to take on something on a more full-time basis, if you feel up to it. You'll find the volunteering staff are trained in making the process as straight-forward as possible and matching you to the most appropriate work using your skills and interests, so it really is made as easy as possible for you. And don't forget the Internet more generally too – here are some fantastic volunteering websites to use as a starting point:

- ✓ www.do-it.org.uk
- ✓ www.volunteering.org.uk
- ✓ www.vinspired.com

Volunteering can really help you discover a new sense of fulfilment in a way you wouldn't normally have expected. You may discover a whole new world you'd completely forgotten about when working – I mean, when do you acknowledge and even remember that the elderly exist and that sometimes they have computer classes that need help in running? Or that there are centres to support asylum seekers adjust to life in the UK and help them cope with issues that they may be facing – some come from war-torn countries and may be suffering from trauma in comprehending their experiences. If you do remember those who need help, then that's great :). I just know how easy it is to forget the wider community around you and the way this evolves with the fantastic work that volunteers do when you are burrowed away in your own busy, complicated life...

So get out there and help others, whilst also helping yourself! Plus, you never know what kind of avenues volunteering may open up for you – you may absolutely love the work you do and want to change careers! You never know. Or perhaps it'll offer you the kind of reward you really enjoy, and you decide to continue volunteering once your Time Away from the Norm comes to an end, and continue to make a difference. Or perhaps it will just be a really nice experience that you remember and take away with you and pass onto others. And even if it is just that, then surely it's worth giving it a shot?

Offering your Services (not quite so Literally...!)

The UK is often criticised for having a lacking sense of community; people don't know their neighbours, the very people that live around them etc etc – you know the drill – you've heard it all before. However much you agree with this, or not, having Time Away from the Norm can really help you reconnect with those that live within close proximity of you. The key here, along with the rest of this guide, is really just trying and giving it a go. Your gesture can be as minute or as big as you like – whatever you're comfortable with and whatever you feel like doing at the time. So, for example, if it's snowing outside, perhaps you could help pick up a few groceries or clear the front drive for an elderly neighbour – you'll be surprised at how many old people really struggle in such weather conditions and often end up becoming housebound due to fear of slipping over in the ice. Not just old people, mind. I lose count of the number of times I slip and fall over when it's icy – it's snow joke! But anyway, simple gestures like this can make all the difference, and it's worth having a think about those that live near you and how you can help them out in some shape or form. So get that thinking cap on and bring out the Samaritan in you!

Help Good Ol' Dave

Yep, that's right; this involves helping those people in your life that you already know. This is also a great option if volunteering seems like something that's too difficult for you to try at the moment; if perhaps you're feeling a tad unsure about it or if you simply don't fancy it. But why and how can you help those you already know? Well, you'll be really surprised at how many people around you need a bit of help sometimes. You may know someone who's getting married and has such little time that they don't know their favours from their flowers. You may know someone who's frantically revising for exams, but needs a bit of help with their CV and cover letter for when they complete their Masters. Perhaps there's someone who's working full-time and their child-minder has the flu. Or someone's gone on holiday and needs a pet-sitter for the week. You may know someone whose PC has broken down; they desperately need a new one but just don't have the time to shop around for the best deal going. Perhaps you could lend a hand there. I'm sure you get the picture. And it'll make you feel great for helping – it will give you something tangible and often very substantial to do – give you an idea you may not previously have had, or simply let you relish in the enjoyment and satisfaction of knowing that you helped someone you love and care about. And it most certainly won't be forgotten! And although I don't advocate running around and doing people's chores, shopping and whatnot for them, the key here is noting that everyone needs a little help from time to time, and realising that you can really make a difference by putting in a favour now and then. Have a go ;).

Earn that Blue Peter Badge

Ever wanted to do more for charity, but never really had the time? Fancy doing something fun, but raising money for it at the same time? Whatever it is that you have in mind, fundraising can really boost your energy levels, make you feel good about doing something worthwhile and help to make some kind of difference to the thousands of charities out there, grafting away. These charities can really do with people like me and you. Perhaps you have a charity in mind that means a great deal to you and you'd like to help give them a boost. Maybe a charity helped you or someone close to you and you'd like to give something back to them. Or perhaps the hard work a charity does is something that you've directly been affected by. Whichever and however many charities you have in mind – it's a win-win situation all round, so you really do have nothing to lose. What a fab and generous thing to during your Time Away from the Norm!

In terms of setting up the fundraising event, this can be as simple and straight-forward as you wish – even baking some cakes and selling them amongst friends can work wonders (not only for the stomach!). I remember doing something like this before – it was a 24-hour cakeathon and involved getting cake orders from friends and family who were able to order whichever cake they wanted in advance, and have it customised as they liked. It worked a treat, and despite all the mess(!), stress and general craziness of it all, I managed to raise a good sum of money for two fab charities. And you can do this with anything you're good at baking and making. I remember a guy I went to university with who went by the name of 'Spag-Bol-Dave' – he helped raise a large sum of money for Cancer Research around campus and there's no prize in guessing what his speciality dish was! And you really can do anything! Perhaps you're a whizz at making pancakes, potting plants, boiling eggs or building matchstick pyramids (No?!). Or for further inspiration why not check out the Guinness Book of Records – out there are *the* most random and obscure records that have been broken all over the shop. Now I'm not suggesting that you go away and break a world record a day, but you can absolutely amend and adapt a record to suit what could be a more practical and feasible option for you. Or... you *could* just go away and become a record breaker! And don't forget to get all those around you involved – you'll need lots of sponsors after all, so dig out those contacts and get in touch with everyone – friends, family, colleagues, neighbours, that long, lost aunt out in Utah... everyone :).

A great way to get others involved is to do a type of sporting or team event. Now I'm not talking about doing a full-on running marathon in a big, stuffy Wombles outfit where you can barely breathe, let alone see where you're going from the sheer delusion of it all (I know someone who did this and they said they would *never* do it again!). I'm thinking more a walking marathon, a half marathon jog or a

5k run. These are all achievable lengths and distances that most people, (if they train and prepare accordingly) can achieve. I highly recommend a walking marathon, as they're actually pretty difficult – the sensible people will realise this early on and train accordingly. However, they'll always be others who believe it will be as 'easy as piiiiiie'; don't do any training and then really struggle on the day... doh! One fab marathon that I would advocate is the Beachy Head marathon down in Eastbourne. It takes in the most beautiful and scenic coastal views along the South Downs countryside and cliffs – it's really challenging, but gives you the choice of running, jogging or walking the marathon. So even if there's a big group of you with mixed abilities, you can each choose which method you'd prefer to complete the marathon in. I bag walking every time ;). It's a fantastically organised event and they give you Mars Bars, hot soup, and fruit squash at each of the pit stops, and have some top supporters to cheer you on and keep you going. Hurray! And you can literally get anyone involved in this, get away for the weekend and just generally have a nice time.

And you really don't have to be a sports bod or a baker to raise money for charity. There are lots of alternatives and you may already have your own ideas or seen things that have worked well in the past – so whether this is putting on a charity ball, a game show, a boat party, a games tournament or your own version of the X-Factor – whatever it is – *now's* the chance to make it happen! And even if the event isn't scheduled for another few months, you can get all the groundwork done during your Time Away from the Norm – find a great DJ, sort out any funding, ticketing, guest lists, themes, marketing – all those bits and pieces that often get left until the last minute and then get done in a hurry. Not by you though – you'll have your Time Away from the Norm to help you out with that... fantastic!

Stomp & SHOUT!

I'm sure you see and hear about it on a regular basis, so I don't have to preach to you about all the injustice in our country and generally throughout the world. But sometimes it's time to speak up and act on it. This can be small or big, and as local or as international as you'd like it to be. So perhaps you have strong views about gay rights, animal protection, tuition fees or a new housing estate being built on a beautiful piece of green land in your local area. What are you going to do about it? Talk to everyone you know and tell them how disgusted you are with it? OK, that's fine, that's great. But how about doing something productive and contacting a local group and maybe getting yourself out there – handing out leaflets to inform people, protesting, taking the issue to your local MP? If it's worthy enough for you to get into a huff and a puff about it, then I think it's damn well worth putting energy into something you truly care about, and actually doing something about it.

How many times have you been wronged in terms of a service you paid for which promised you the world, but gave you far from? Purchased something online that turned up and wasn't quite what you ordered? Bought some food which just didn't taste as good as it promised it would...? Well, again it's worth doing something about this! Write a letter, pick up the phone, go to customer services – get something out of it! All too often we dismiss these mistakes and perceive sorting things out as 'too much hassle', or we're all just a bit too polite and not up for the bit of argie-bargie that it may entail. But it's your money at the end of day! And sometimes you can get great freebies as a form of compensation for making the effort in complaining. Not in all cases, of course, but there have been instances where I've known people to receive free products, holidays and flights. That worth your while...?

Make Mr Branson Run!

Remember that school project that you believed had real potential? That time on holiday when you said "wouldn't it be great to set up a coffee place round here?" Or the time when you had that lightning bolt idea in the middle of the night; woke up, wrote it down, but never quite did anything with it...? Well, guess what – now *really* is your chance to dig out those scrap bits of paper – to re-evaluate those ideas again, and maybe see if you can action them – it's your Time Away from the Norm after all! It doesn't have to be anything substantial either – often the smallest and simplest of concepts can be the best. I know someone who cashed in on the vuvuzela phenomenal from the 2010 World Cup in South Africa by ordering a large quantity from China and selling them on. If vuvuzelas aren't quite up your street, it's still great to use this time to explore your ideas and set up some kind of venture. Or at the very least brainstorm and look into the idea – make a few calls and see how feasible and realistic your idea is. And whilst you're using your brain in this way, you'll be surprised at how many other ideas come to you, as you really start to think in a technically creative manner. "But I'm no entrepreneur" you exclaim! Rubbish. No-one needs to be an entrepreneur to have their own business. You just need a bit of common sense and an idea. Oh, and the guts to do something about it. That's important. And before you dismiss it, at least give it a good thinking over. And I look forward to seeing you on the next series of The Apprentice ;)!

And if starting your own business simply isn't viable at this stage, why not pitch your own Dragon's Den night with your friends? You can pick a few chums to impersonate the Dragons (*everyone* has a Duncan Bannatyne lookalike friend – no?!). You don't have to come up with super-fantastic ideas either – maybe just come up with the absolute plain ridiculous (the sillier, the better!) and just have a really fun night in. On that note – why not create your own version of other TV shows that float your boat that you and your friends enjoy watching? Your own rendition of Total Wipeout, Play Your Cards Right or Big Brother! OK, perhaps not Big Bro ;).

Enrol on a Course

There are so many part-time courses out there, I had no idea! As mentioned in *'Get a Hobby'* (chapter 4), you may have an old hobby or interest you'd like to reclaim and reconnect with again, or you may fancy trying out something new. If so, why not do a course on it? CityLit is an adult education centre that comes to mind in central London, but there really are thousands of institutions offering courses all around the country – best thing is to do a local search. You could even be an eager beaver and spend time working towards a degree or another career. If you can't find anything appropriate or at a time that suits, don't worry, as you can always sign up for a course starting in the future, but use the time meanwhile to do some preparation for this.

This could be practising your yoga and aerobics skills through a DVD if you're looking to do a fitness course, to going out and having a go at your local climbing centre before embarking on an outdoor climbing course, for example. And don't forget the option of distance learning online – this is one of the most flexible ways to study, and is really worth exploring if you're after that bit of ease and convenience.

I did a couple of courses during my Time Away from the Norm and found the benefits to be endless; I met amazing like-minded people, realised I had strengths away from the workplace and found new hobbies that I'll be continuing with in the future. When you're working full-time, it often occurs that you forget that you have skills and assets outside of work, or even if you knew that you had these talents, when was the last time you thought to utilise them? A course can also help you re-gain some of the confidence you may have recently lost, and this is a great way to do just that. In fact, this is one of my most highly rated areas – definitely give it a go, and you'll understand what I'm talking about ;).

WFH

Now we're not talking about the World Federation of Haemophilia here, we're talking about Working From Home, which involves doing your usual work, but from home. And as with any of the pointers in this guide, this may be the very last thing on your mind, and this is completely fine and understandable. However, if you're anything like me, you may be itching to get back into the swing of things as soon as possible, and working from home is a really great way to ease you back into the way of working, particularly if you've been off work for a lengthy period of time. One of the fantastic things about doing this is that it really lets you go at your own pace, as it's totally within your control – you can do as much or as little as you like. You can even do dummy tasks if you really wish and adamantly insist on having no pressure put on you. Or perhaps you can do some research or write up something that would be interesting to help or share with your team or organisation. A unique idea you have perhaps. Normally these type of additions are 'nice to have's' in any company; work that would often get side-lined as resources need to be prioritised elsewhere. But now you have this fantastic opportunity do something a bit different, which is still very relevant and can even help make a difference to your workplace. Brilliant :).

It is also a great opportunity to gain some feedback on the work you do, and if you find that working from home is helping you, you can build up the hours to resemble that of a typical working day or week, if you like. This is also especially useful if you're not being paid for your time off work, as this could be a way to enable you to be paid, as well as helping to phase you back into working life again. Maybe give it a whirl to see how it goes. If things don't pan out, at least it's an option you've tried, and perhaps it's something you can try again at a later stage, or alternatively have a go at some other work-related ideas in this chapter.

Career Self-Audit Time

You don't have to be unhappy in your job or even be considering leaving to be thinking of future moves and updating your CV. Your CV is an important document to keep updated, as often we forget about the ever-crucial things we do on a day-to-day basis at work that we sometimes dismiss or simply forget to add in. Whilst updating your CV, it's also worth scouring the job market for your potential future job. Maybe put together a 'wish list' of companies that you'd like to work for. Again, even if you're not looking, it doesn't hurt to have a look at a role you could do in say a year or so's time, and look at the core skills, experiences and competencies required for the role and how you can progress into it from where you are now. Taking note of this can enable you to see where you are heading in your own role and to help you gain and improve the skills right now for tomorrow's job. It also keeps you on your toes, as you never know what's around the corner. *Particularly* in today's economic climate. Plus, when you are ready to make that leap and change jobs, you'll be one step ahead of the game and can crack right on with it! And if you're not quite content with your job, then these are the first crucial steps you'll need to have in place for any kind of move, regardless. And if you're having a bit of a career self-audit and realise that you'd like to have a bit of a change from what you are currently doing, then have a sneaky look ahead to chapter 11 where I look at this in more detail ;).

Arena's Top-Tip Chapter Summary

✓ Add your positive notions to the world by doing some volunteer work – short-term or long-term – your help is needed!

✓ Help those in your local community by putting yourself out there and seeing what you can do to help – even the smallest of gestures soon add up

✓ There'll always be someone you know who can do with a helping hand that will be vastly appreciated and long remembered

✓ Use your time off to set up a fundraiser to raise money for some well-deserved charities and really help make a difference to them

✓ It's time to speak up about the injustices you experience and witness – now's the time to get your viewpoint out there and to do something about it!

✓ Have a go at putting that lightning bolt idea into practice and maybe set up your own business during your time off – why not?

✓ Take up a course, and use this as a formal way to structure your time off and learn more about something you're interested in

✓ Gently ease back into the ways of the working world by working from home and doing some simple tasks to begin with

✓ Do a bit of a career self-audit by getting your CV up-to-date, and just generally having a think about your working life

10. Back To Work

So you're due to return back to work. You've met with your doctor, spoken to occupational health and had a meeting with your line manager, your manager's manager, your manager's manager's hamster and HR. And after climbing through all those hoops and hurdles, you've been given the all-OK to return to work – hurray and well done! You've gotten this far :). You may have mixed feelings about going back to work – perhaps you're excited about seeing your colleagues again, but also nervous about how you'll cope with the normal day-to-day grind of the working Norm again. Whatever your concerns, this next chapter looks to cover some of these issues and help make this move as seamless as possible for you ;).

Go Let it Out!

Wahoo, you're due back to work next week! You're excited about seeing everyone again, getting back to some good ol' grafting and having your old schedule firmly back in hand. You also feel rested and relaxed – ready for the challenge of work again: bring-it-on. But for some, I know, it may not be all fun and games – you could be having concerns about how you will cope with going back to your usual workload, what people may say and think, how you will deal with that new billing system that's been introduced while you've been off, and most importantly – what if it happens again...? A great way to get over these initial concerns is to write them all down – there's no point in them going round and round in your head, and it's far more productive to let them out now versus worrying about them at 2.56am in the middle of the night. So whether it's a small concern or even a tiny concern – write it out. At the end of the day, if it's something that's worrying you and making you anxious, then it's well worth writing it out and addressing it. It may even be quickly resolvable, so won't it feel great to cross it off your list? OK, so you have your list of concerns and worries. Now what? Well it's worth having a think and working out who will be the best person to help you with these issues – maybe a trusted friend or partner would be suitable for some of these, whereas other points may be better dealt with through your line manager, HR or even a friend at work. Whoever it is, it's worth getting in touch with them and just generally sorting them out as soon as possible, as essentially it will benefit all parties in resolving these apprehensions. Plus, if it gives you some kind of peace of mind, then I think it's definitely worth that call.

Maybe you don't have a list of tangible concerns as such, but are nevertheless feeling pretty nervous. That's completely understandable. A great way to boost your confidence here is by writing a list of all the good things about your workplace that you remember or some happy memories that you have of the place. I recall doing this at one stage, and you'll be surprised at the randomness of the memories, and also at how naturally the list comes about. Memories could include a great park that you go to for lunch, a fantastic pepperoni sandwich filling at your local deli (hey, food's important!) or any comical stories of things that have happened either in the office or at a work-related social event – whatever it is that makes you smile or laugh about work – jot it down. Perhaps create a work-related version of your 'Inspiration' book to add and refer to when needed. This is a sure way to boost your confidence and get into a positive frame of mind in terms of returning to work. Have a go at it ;).

Informally Meet

Seeing some work-related folks before returning to the office can make all the difference in how you feel. So perhaps a quiet drink with a couple of frolleagues that you trust before you go back may help to reassure and make the whole journey back that bit easier. You can catch-up on any news or goss and perhaps fix in a lunch date with them for your first day back, so however your first morning goes, you'll have your lunch break sorted and can look forward to this going well. Maybe also tell them about your concerns in what people might say – this may enable them to act as allies to help ease off any unwanted attention on your first day back and generally so. And if you're not too friendly with your work colleagues or simply don't wish to see them, perhaps if you've been allocated a mentor from a different team at work, it may be worth meeting with them if you feel more comfortable doing this. Again, they're likely to be happy to help and a quick drink could work in exactly the same way. If you still don't fancy seeing anyone – maybe just drop an email to a couple of people from work – this could work just as well. The key is to have that bit of informal communication to help make you feel at ease with those you work with.

Another useful person worth meeting up with before you return to work is your line manager. Perhaps in a more informal outlet like a café than in the harsher confines of the office environment. Plus you're both on mutual grounds then and it's more likely to feel relaxed – perfect for an open and honest chat. And if your manager tends to resemble Cruella over Snow White or has more in common with the likes of Dracula than Mr Incredible, it really is still worth making the effort and putting the offer out there. The likelihood is that they'll accept. And if you've had your differences before, then now really is the time to make amends – you'll need them to be on your side and to help support you back to work. If it's a real no-no from their side, or they just genuinely don't have the time – try another member of your team; an alternative supervisor or perhaps an old manager within the organisation that you had a better relationship with. And if you've always gotten on well with your manager, then fab – coffee meeting in the diary.

When meeting with your manager it's worth bringing along any concerns that you have about returning to work, and going over any changes that have occurred in the workplace since you were last about – any new people, systems, protocols, seating arrangements, projects, clients etc. Whatever it is, it's worth getting a heads up before you return so you can be as informed and ready as possible. It's also worth discussing how you've been doing and checking what your and your line manager's expectations are in terms of workload, and ensuring that you're both on the same page in terms of these estimations. For instance, if you're expecting to work on the same number of projects as you previously had, whereas your manager was thinking half would be more realistic, then it's well worth having that conversation. This way you're clear about what level of performance is required from you. However, I do appreciate that it does depend on where you work and the type of work you do, as each workplace is different – so it's worth clarifying and exploring all angles most relevant to you and your workplace to ensure that everything is crystal. And remember – you always have a say in this, so do voice what you think is reasonable and not! Now's the perfect opportunity for this...

Another point worth talking over is your action plan and how you've been progressing with this – and perhaps creating a new one (or adding in a couple more slides) to help ease you back as seamlessly as possible. To make monitoring progress a regular occurrence – maybe set a weekly review date to check how things are going – what's working well, what isn't working so well and what can be learnt from these experiences and put into practice for the following week. Constantly updating and ensuring that you and your manager are both on the same wavelength is crucial here, as this will really help make it easier in terms of getting you back to work.

Another source of ammunition to have is to discuss why you were originally signed off work and how this can be prevented in the future. This will be entirely dependent on why you were signed off initially, but if for instance you were suffering with panic attacks, it may be worth speaking about how these can be minimised. It should also be accepted that these attacks may still continue to occur, but it's worth implementing some ideas on how these can be reduced. So for example putting in place a 'survival kit', which may include paper bags, stress balls, soothing drops – whatever's worked for you in the past or any new ideas that you now have – get this sorted!

Once you've had this chat with your manager, have a think about others in your workplace – is there anyone else that you could benefit from having a chat with? Now is not the time for coyness, and if you deem that there's someone else that can make a difference in how you feel about returning to work or can reassure you, then these conversations are well worth having. So start pencilling in! The aim is to feel as calm, informed and prepared as possible.

Those Initial Convo's

So it's your first day back in the office. People are staring at you and shifting about uncomfortably. Or so it seems. Yes, people will notice that you're back and that you've been away for a while. This is normal. People may approach you and ask you how you are, and it's entirely up to you how much detail you wish to go into – 'I'm doing much better now, thanks' or a 'it's good to be back' is sufficient. It may appear that they're not being very tactful when they ask you questions or that they're acting nosy – they may be, but nine times out of ten they're just genuinely concerned for you and happy to have you back. It may be the case that they don't know what to say to you; they don't want to upset you by saying the wrong thing or they're not entirely sure how to act around you – and naturally some people may find this more difficult than others. Try to see it from their perspective too – it's not easy knowing what the 'right' thing to say is. And as scary as it may seem to you, it's *far* likely to be scarier for them! If you're concerned about their responses, then maybe look to ask questions about things that are important to them to break away any tension and to deflect attention away from yourself. People are always happy to speak about their kids, pets and upcoming holidays for instance – so give one of those topics a whirl – your colleagues will feel at ease and so will you, hence making future conversations that bit easier. And yes, this is a tough part of returning back to work, but it's over very quickly – people's attention is diverted quickly, and you will soon become yesterday's news in no time! And if anyone is genuinely making you feel uncomfortable and being outright rude and intrusive, then remember that you don't have to tell them anything at all – it was your Time Away from the Norm after all, not theirs :).

Give it a Chance

OK, so you've been back at work a few days now, things are ticking along OK, and you've overcome those initial difficult conversations. However, it just doesn't feel right... This again is really quite normal. I remember returning to the office expecting things to be very different, and in fact it seemed that people had remained rooted to their seats the whole time I'd been away – it felt extremely odd. I'm not sure what I was expecting exactly, but it wasn't that. And I guess on the other hand if you expect things to be the same, and actually there are lots of new faces, changes in seating arrangements and different processes in place, then this too can be unsettling and can take a while to get used to. Depending on your working environment, it may also feel bizarre being fairly grounded to your seat all day, when you may have become accustomed to wandering around quite freely in your Time Away from the Norm. This again is understandable. And remember that whatever your expectations are, as with any – they may be different to reality, and that you do need to be patient and flexible and give it a fair chance to get used to again. Your life for the past few weeks, months or years has been very different, and getting used to the more rigid routine of office life can be difficult to adjust to, but here the saying 'patience is a virtue' could not be more appropriate. Readjust your expectations early on and remember to take each day as it comes – one day may be a breeze, but another may be a whole different tug of war. So remember to take things very slowly to begin with until you establish some type of routine, and you're back up to speed and in your element again. Just keep in mind that it really does take time, and to give it the fair chance that it deserves.

Put in Place a Contingency Plan

I love a bit of contingency. It always pays to put some in place, whatever you are doing. In this case the contingency refers to the reason why you were signed off work, and doing your utmost to ensure that you can avoid the situation from occurring again. This may in fact be your greatest concern, and again, this is entirely reasonable. Fear not! A good way to catch this is to make a list of all the early warning signs you felt last time and to keep tabs on whether these signs reappear at any stage. These signs can be absolutely anything from catastrophising, feeling resentful towards others, being tenser, feeling more tired, getting angry, not eating properly to drinking more alcohol – literally any indicators that you felt before. Maybe you can rank these signs in terms of severity. Recording these in your journal could also be a useful way of keeping an eye on these tell-tale signs. If any of them resurface then it's worth looking at your current situation, speaking to your manager or HR and making some amends. And don't wait for the symptoms to build up or disregard them if you feel that there have only been a couple of them – they're called early warning signs for a reason! They put you in your situation last time, so do not ignore them if they reappear again. Note, if your self-perception skills aren't always tip-top then get others you trust to take note and gently let you know if you're slipping. The key here is that you're doing everything you possibly can to ensure you don't go down the same path again. You know how tough it can be, and although I know that you can handle it, let's try not to go there again.

It's also worth having some kind of plan in place if these early warning signs do appear. These can be work related, so flagging up to your manager that you're not feeling so great, and that your feelings aren't dissimilar to when you were initially signed off work. It's in your manager's interest to know this and to help in whichever way they can. Maybe embedded in this plan there are things that you can do for yourself to help you feel better – going for a swim, seeing a friend, starting a creative project, taking out unnecessary events from your week and prioritising the essentials to ensure maximum R&R time. You'll know by now what works best for you, as hopefully you would have worked out a few key de-stressing exercises during your Time

Away from the Norm. Ultimately, having a contingency plan provides confidence and ammunition – so keep this at hand!

If it still doesn't feel Right

Now you've been back a while – be it a few weeks or months, and you've been patient, you've given it a chance, however things still feel difficult and just aren't improving. You've genuinely tried. Remember at this stage to remain open and honest with yourself, and perhaps discuss this with your line manager, HR or occupational health – there may be other options available for you to try. A phased return to work could help, for instance, or possibly splitting your work between your home and the office and gradually increasing office hours over time. Whatever it is, it's worth having the conversations to see if there's another option and another way – remember that the more heads knocked together, the greater the brain power!

After trying these options, it's worth considering that perhaps a bit more time off work might be what you need. This may be a daunting concept initially, and one which may be quite difficult to accept. However, try to look at it on a longer term perspective – another couple of weeks or months off work is nothing in the grand scheme of the rest of the year, the next ten years or the rest of your career or life. Plus remember not to be too hard on yourself – it cannot be stressed enough that recovery is a _process_ and that it takes time – it doesn't simply happen overnight or in the duration of your time off work, and it's imperative to realise this and to continue to work hard at it. Keep going! It's also important to bear in mind that you were never going to know how you would feel about being back at work until you actually tried it. So don't just see it as 'Oh-My-God – _more_ time off!' – instead think of all that you've learnt about yourself during your time off – the skills and hobbies you've developed – not to mention all that you've learnt and discovered about yourself and your development more generally – all of which will serve you well for the rest of your life. Truly – don't forget that.

And at the end of the day – remember not to lose sight of the bigger picture – it's really only work – it is not the be all and end all, and that there are other things _far_ more important than the '9 to 5.' So as important as work is – try not to lose perspective of the bigger world around us! Oh, and keep on going :).

Arena's Top-Tip Chapter Summary

✓ Let out your woes and concerns, and look to clarify and resolve these before you head back to work

✓ Perhaps meet with your manager or another trusted work colleague to catch-up and fully prepare for your return

✓ Remember that your first day back won't last forever, and it's worth having some conversation topics ready to make it that bit easier with colleagues

✓ As tough as it is, remember that adjusting back to work does take time, and to give it the time and patience it deserves

✓ To avoid getting into a similar situation of having time off again, put into place a contingency plan to spot those tell-tale signs from resurfacing

✓ If things still don't feel right being back at work, do look to explore other options within your workplace which could pan out instead

11. If Things Don't Work Out...

...then that's OK! Really, it is :). Often things happen for a reason, and if you do decide that your current situation of being away from work or going to work (or maybe the yo-yo effect of being in and out of work) is causing you more stress than you'd bargained for, and that you are feeling worse as a result, then sometimes it's OK to leave things be and to walk away. You would in no way be a failure. In fact, quite the opposite; you've noticed that things are not working out, and you are doing something about it. Now **_that_** takes some real guts and courage, believe me ;).

The EAP & ACAS

What's with the acronyms you ask? Well, as I've mentioned, I'm not claiming to have all the answers. Simply because I don't have them. But what I do have are my experiences, and based on these I have two helplines that I would very much like to recommend to you. The first being the Employee Assistance Programme. A large number of organisations have one of these programmes in place, and you can get their telephone number from your work Intranet, through your line manager, HR or simply via another colleague or your company switchboard. Do not fret if your company doesn't have an EAP provider – ask around; you'll be surprised at how many of your family members, friends, housemates and others you know have access to one and will have a number available for you to call. Failing that – Google it (but I didn't tell you that, of course...!). Now the EAP have a helpline that you can call and they put you through to one of their trained counsellors who are absolutely fantastic to speak to. One of my reasons for giving you only two contacts is that the EAP have a giant directory of other organisations and charities that could potentially help you and point you in the right direction, if needed. If you are going through a bereavement, for example, they can give you suitable and relevant contacts. Depending on the type of programme your organisation has, the level of support may vary, but at the very least they will have a series of trained counsellors for you to speak to about any type of issue you might have. Other programmes may be able to offer face-to-face counselling or online help in the form of factsheets, case studies and other written information.

ACAS, on the other hand, are very different to the EAP in that they help both employers and employees avoid and resolve employee issues. They offer advice, are very sympathetic and if you are seeking information on employment rights and rules or just generally want a heads up on where you currently stand, then they are really worth giving a buzz. They are contactable Monday to Friday 8am – 8pm on 08457 47 47 47 (www.acas.org.uk) and can offer you some true peace of mind. Try them.

Now the next hurdle: I know you may not feel like calling either of them. You may think that they won't understand you. You may have 101 different reasons for why you don't wish to call either of them. I know I certainly used to. And quite rightly so. Why should you call a complete stranger and tell them all about your troubles and woes...? However, the key here is to have their numbers at hand for when you do want them – you don't have to know when this time will be, but it's simply worth having the numbers saved in your phone or at home for when a call to either is exactly what you need. You may have your own numbers for helplines that you'd prefer to call – this again is absolutely fine. It's important to remember that such phonelines are completely confidential and even if you feel that your problems aren't very big, it's crucial to realise that helplines can be used even for the smallest of problems – because at the end of the day, if there's something that's causing you distress or concern, then it's absolutely worth talking through. Call them – you'll be surprised. I know I was. And don't forget that this is your Time Away from the Norm – you are living out a new routine; a new Norm which involves doing the things you *wouldn't normally do*. And that's just to remind you – in case you needed another reason to call them ;).

Self-help

The shelves out there are brimming with self-help books promising you a better way to live your life, ultimate happiness and all things brilliant and improved. I know it may be easy to be cynical about these, but now I say: 'don't knock it until you've tried it.' If you've knocked it before, it's probably because you didn't actually need self-help. Perhaps you just read them out of curiosity to see what all the fuss was about. And they still didn't really apply. The reality is that some books are just meant to be read in the moment. And when they are, they can have real impact. Not all books, I agree. But sometimes just the right book at the right time can really inspire you to make changes and take action on your life. A book that I personally found to be very inspiring is 'Who Stole My Mojo?' by Gary Bertwistle, which is an especially motivating read – it really made me want to get up and do something, and certainly helped me to go out and reclaim my Mojo back. And I'd actually recommend the book to absolutely anyone, regardless of whether they're having Time Away from the Norm or not. Another fab guide, a type of 'been there, done that' type guide that offers pure and simple advice on life's peaks and troughs is a book by Lesley Garner called 'Life's Lessons' – a really great, straight-forward read. But anyhow, maybe stroll along to your local library or bookstore and take a look at some of the books on offer to see what stands out and catches your eye. Or maybe if you've had self-help books recommended in the past, but you shrugged these off at the time... well now's the time to go back and change that by taking those people up on their offer. People don't tend to rave about their favourite self-help book for no reason, after all! Well, I know I certainly don't anyway ;).

Online courses can also be a fantastic way to help yourself in a really easy and convenient manner. One that I would personally recommend is called 'Living Life to the Full' (www.llttf.com). This is based on Cognitive Behavioural Therapy principles and provides a free set of 'life skills' to anyone that logs onto their site, as well as a free Hospital Anxiety and Depression test and Patient Health Questionnaire test, which you can take as often as you like to assess your mood. This is great as it can highlight quite quickly how you are doing (through taking the tests) and perhaps enable you to seek further help, should this be required. You can work on the different modules at completely your own pace, and take the ones that you feel are most relevant to you. Or try them all. Maybe you can stick one a week into your timetable or schedule for a set time so that you keep this learning at a constant. Now, I'm not in a position to be recommending any type of therapy to anyone, but I believe that this course can benefit absolutely anyone. And when I say anyone, I really do mean just that. It's a very goal-orientated approach, and it really does teach you skills for life that you can learn and apply to all areas of your life. I believe that it can actually help improve you – if you're willing to be open and to be improved, so to speak. The course modules cover all types of topics and problem areas that anyone may suffer with from time to time, but perhaps more so when you're experiencing Time Away from the Norm. So whatever your story, and whatever other help you're receiving, this tool (along with many others that I'm sure exist) are well worth having a go at, and you'll soon be recognising when your new found skills become habitual and a part of who you are. What an incredibly amazing gain to make during your Time Away from the Norm!

And don't forget that there are *so* many alternatives out there in terms of help and support – one-to-one therapy, support groups, holistic approaches, expressive therapies – so much – and you won't know what's right for you until you look into them, and decide which would be best for you as an individual. And remember that absolutely everyone struggles from time to time – doctors, counsellors, therapists and many others – and as corny (and perhaps mortifying) as it may sound, it really is all simply part of being a human being :).

Get a Life Coach

Sometimes when you are having Time Away from the Norm, you may be looking for a little direction in your life to guide you along the way. You may be looking for inspiration to help you think outside the box and to get that Oomph back in you again. Life coaches are people that can help you do this, and although sometimes costly, they can help you achieve things a lot quicker than if you tried to do it yourself, particularly if you are not totally yourself at the moment. There are also opportunities to use coaches that have a sliding scale of rates, and can therefore be more affordable, as well as those that are training to coach and could even offer you free sessions. Do note though that they are in no way substitutes for doctors or therapists, as they deal with a whole different kettle of fish. So do bear this in mind. But otherwise, if you'd like to look to your future, prioritise your goals and ultimately achieve them, then a life coach could certainly help form a part of the answer.

Think about what you want... (what you really, really want)

It's tough. I'll be the first to admit that. But it's important to be realistic about what you want and realise that it takes time – ideas aren't going to come to you in the flash of an instance or merely overnight – they take some thinking, pondering and then some more thinking. So if you're at a bit of a crossroads with where your life is heading, then that really is OK. It's pretty normal actually. And the really great thing is that there's a lot you can do about it!

Firstly, it's worth finding out what techniques work best for you – you may be a list person and wish to write down all the things you wish to achieve on a short, medium and long term basis, and then to look at all the pros and cons in achieving these goals and how your current options feed into these. That's just one idea. And speaking of goals, this is an area that I've always been very guilty of shying away from. But there was a reason for this, and it took a wise old cracker to change my habits. The cracker told me that goals can be as small and minute as you want them to be. Sound simple? Well, this changed everything for me! I always envisaged goals to be really big – 'bungee jump, do a triathlon and then climb Ben Nevis' style and for that reason never really bothered to set any. But now I know that anything from getting through a social event to finding a temporary job can all be objectives. And I think goals really help when experiencing Time Away from the Norm. I didn't set any during my time off, but know now that they would have really helped me – they give you a sense of focus and achievement, no matter how small. Goals also give you direction – at least you are going *somewhere* and you're not just stuck in orbit in the middle of limbo-land. Definitely set some!

If you're a more visual person, you may find it useful to do a mind map going from one idea to another, and really stemming out from each point and examining what you'd like in various areas of your life. The best way to make the most of this technique is to scribble the first thing that comes to mind and to keep going from there and see where it spontaneously leads you. The mind map can be as big or as small as you like and focus on whatever angle you'd like to look at. This can be just one idea at a time or several different ones. I remember taping nine A4 sheets of paper together to solely look at which creative projects I wanted to work on in the next month. And there really are hundreds of different techniques out there that you can use to help you with your exploration and thinking, and www.mindtools.com is an absolutely fantastic website which demonstrates lots of different approaches that you can try and utilise. You could even combine several together – do check it out.

Maybe your greatest ideas come to you in the middle of the night or whilst on a dull bus journey into town. If this is the case, then it's worth keeping a notebook handy and writing down absolutely anything that you discover and think about during the day (and night!)

– what you'd like to be doing, what you currently don't like doing, what environments you enjoy and feel relaxed in, when you feel at your happiest, what excites you and grabs your attention, elements of what you can see yourself doing – literally *any* ideas that come to mind – however silly or impractical they may appear at the time – jot them down! Normally there is some kind of serious undertone to them; they wouldn't just randomly come to mind otherwise, would they? Again, your ideal is unlikely to come to you immediately, but a notebook is a really useful way to get into the habit of regularly thinking about ideas and jotting them down.

Another thing: going back to your core values and beliefs could not be further underrated. We all have a set of values and beliefs that make up who we are, what we believe in and ultimately what we see as 'right' or 'wrong.' They help us dictate how we view the world, and represent our highest beliefs. Without them, we wouldn't be who we are. So whatever your core values are, (and we all have them), look at these at the outset and use them as a basis for your thinking in what you'd like to be doing. So if for example one of your greatest values is 'freedom', and you're working in a very rigid and structured environment, then this could be causing you some distress. If you value 'ambition', and you're working in a place where promotion, for whatever reason, just isn't happening, then this is also likely to be a bit of a stressor. It may sound really basic, but core values are so frequently overlooked, and it's a wonder why people don't feel content in their jobs, as they're forcing themselves to work for organisations where their core beliefs don't match. Consequently they end up causing themselves unhappiness and resentment as they try to mould themselves into something that they're not, instead of looking for something that's a better fit for them. Catch my drift?

As well as going back to your core values and jotting down any thoughts or ideas that spring to mind, it's also worth writing down all your achievements, talents and skills – anything that you've accomplished in the past – however big or small it was. This is a fab way to really identify (and remind yourself!) what you can do and have done, and allows you to examine the type of skill-set that you have. Your achievements can be work-related or personal – so something you did when you were at school, scouts, work, holiday – jot it down and make it count. So whether it's the fact that you know how to drive

114

a car, and you really enjoy this. 'So what?' you question, but actually this could mean something and you may wish to implement this in your future job role. Perhaps it highlights your logical mind. Maybe it emphasises independence, freedom and the need to travel. Whatever it means to you and however you decide to read and interpret it – take note! It may not be overly apparent in the first instance, but over time as you continue with your research, you'll begin to notice patterns and recurring themes in your notes. You'll also become used to making these associations as you become familiar and used to doing such exercises. And it's funny how rationalising and reflecting like this is so important, yet we allocate such little time to thinking about what we truly want. Not you and I, obviously ;).

Another good way to get the mind thinking about what you want is by browsing through job vacancies in newspapers or online, and looking at jobs that could be of potential interest to you – or maybe just elements of different jobs that sound appealing. This helps you build up a portfolio of what you'd like to be doing, as well as enabling you to see the demand in a field of work that you may be interested in doing. If perhaps you're lucky enough to come across a role that you really love, but it's not quite right for you now – maybe you need an additional qualification, for example, it's still worth giving the organisation a call and finding out more about the role and what type of skills and personal qualities they're looking for, for instance. This then gives you a good idea of exactly what you need to work on to achieve your goal of bagging that ideal job!

The UK government's Next Step careers helpline and services (www.nextstep.direct.gov.uk) is another brilliant resource for those looking to discuss their options with someone impartial, and can be contacted on 0800 100 900 during the hours of 8am to 10pm every day of the week. The career coaches are amazing and work through your objectives with you, and then at the end of the call send you a summary and an agreed action plan for you to work on. Depending on your call, the career coach may set you tasks to complete, which could include speaking to certain people regarding your choices. They can also schedule in a call-back with you at an agreed date and time to see how you're getting on, if you wish. Email communication and face-to-face meetings are also available if this is more convenient for you or if you simply prefer these methods. And they really do provide support for a whole range of people – regardless of how senior you may be or if you feel that the work you do is highly specialised and niche – so don't let reasons like this put you off trying them. Plus, it's sometimes just nice to speak freely with someone neutral and objective about your ideas, as often speaking with someone close to you may be difficult; your idea of a complete career change can have an impact upon their life too. And the excellent professional service is available for free – and as often as you like – fantastic!

And don't forget those around you too! Asking your friends, family and colleagues in whichever way you feel comfortable is a really simple, but hugely effective way to gain some insight on yourself that you may otherwise have been a bit short-sighted to. This can be done as simply as sending out an email to as few or as many people as you feel happy with, and asking them questions like what they perceive to be your key personality traits, your strengths and weaknesses, as well as what they see you doing in your career. It's absolutely worth giving it a go, even just for the curiosity aspect of it. But in actual fact you may end up being quite surprised by the extent of insight other people can offer you and how valuable this can be. Even if it's just ideas here and there or certain traits that people have noticed about you – it's great to receive this so you can see how it ties in with your own thoughts and ideas. And you never know, it may bring about the perfect career option for you – now I bet that's worth sending an email out for!

As you can see, this is quite a list and it is by no means exhaustive. These are just *some* pointers which may help – and you may have your own approaches and techniques that you may wish to use in isolation or alongside some of my suggestions. Whatever works best for you really. The main point though is that it does take time, as essentially it is allowing you to think about options that you may not have previously considered. What's good is to be as open and explorative as you can be and to try to get as much out of the exercises as you can. Even if it's a great big list of what you *don't* want in your life, then at least you know what you won't be looking for and can cross those off your list! And still if you do go back to your old field of work, as you've come to realise that what you were previously doing really wasn't so bad, but perhaps needed a bit of tweaking here and there to make it more ideal, then that's also fine! In reality, *where* you work is not going to represent your entire industry, so sometimes just realising that can make a huge difference.

So whatever you end up doing – whether it's taking a few months out of your life or a lot longer, the important thing to remember is that you have to take your time in feeling better about who you are and what you want, and absolutely no-one else can set a time limit on this. And ultimately whatever happens, you'll be OK, you will be just fine – and it'll be a damn sight better than how things used to be :).

A Final Note...

Being signed off work may feel like the be all and end all; you may be in a place you've never been before – somewhere where you can't clearly see the wood for the trees – experiences you've never encountered before. That's OK. It may feel harrowing, frustrating, lonely or just generally plain awful. Again, that's OK. You may undergo a whole mixture of emotions; place blame, feel angry, become self-destructive or just find yourself a bit lost. You will find your way. Someone once told me that feeling these different emotions is actually excellent. I didn't agree with her at the time, but can now see where she was coming from. Feeling the same, normal emotions that you experience on an average day-to-day basis won't get you anywhere. It'll get you so far, sure, but then what? For those of us *lucky* enough to experience Time Away from the Norm, we can feel a variety of things, and then actually use this to our advantage by channelling the excess energy from these emotions in a positive way in helping us achieve what we truly want in life. Brilliant.

Hopefully with this guide, you'll see that there is a world of opportunity out there, and that there really is a lot that can be accomplished and achieved during your Time Away from the Norm. If you want to that is. There's got to be a want, and if there is, you're likely to get through it by using this guide as a starting base.

And the rest of it... well that's up to you... ;). Good luck!

Arena's Top-Tip Chapter Summary

✓ The EAP and ACAS are two organisations who can really provide some sound advice and support during your time off

✓ Help is out there, and you can aid yourself via books, online courses, support groups and alternative therapies

✓ Sometimes getting a life coach can help speed up the process in helping you get what you want and ultimately achieving your potential

✓ Put some time aside to properly think and figure things out – I can assure you this will be the best investment of your time in a long while

✓ Your time off work is really not the be all and end all, and in fact can truly be a blessing. But it really does take you and you only to figure that out – good luck ;)!

12. Resources

Here are a list of resources that have been cited throughout the guide, in order of mention:

Internet

www.gumtree.com
www.meetup.com
www.lulu.com
www.lastminute.com
www.musicmagpie.co.uk
www.wwoof.org
www.couchsurfing.org
www.casitaverde.com
www.showfilmfirst.com
www.england.fm
www.cinnamon.org.uk
www.do-it.org.uk
www.volunteering.org.uk
www.vinspired.com
www.acas.org.uk
www.llttf.com
www.mindtools.com
www.nextstep.direct.gov.uk

Books

Inspiration Book – this is to be created by you, the reader ☺

Guinness Book of Records 2011 (2010) Guinness World Records Limited

Bertwistle, G. (2009) *Who Stole My Mojo?: How to Get it Back and Live, Work and Play Better,* Capstone

Garner, L. (2009) *Life Lessons: Things I Wish I'd Learned Earlier: Pages from a Notebook,* Hay House UK

Questions, thoughts or simply wish to get in touch? Do so by emailing Mali Arena at time.away.from.the.norm@hotmail.co.uk